1000
QUESTIONS
and
ANSWERS

Written by
**John Cooper, Richard Tames,
Margarette Lincoln, Roger Coote,
Laura Wade, Dick File and Harry Ford**

Edited by
**Kay Barnham, Nicola Wright,
Paul Harrison and Hazel Songhurst**

BARNES
&NOBLE
BOOKS
NEW YORK

Contents

DINOSAURS 4

What are dinosaurs? • Where did dinosaurs live? • Which dinosaurs were found first?
What did dinosaurs look like? • What did dinosaurs eat? • Could dinosaurs run?
Could dinosaurs swim? • Could dinosaurs fly? • Did dinosaurs have babies?
Were dinosaurs stupid? • How did their bodies work? • How do you find a dinosaur?
How do you become an expert? • What happened to dinosaurs?

ANCIENT TIMES 32

Where did civilization begin? • Where is the Indus Valley? • What is a dynasty?
When did American civilization begin? • Were there cities in Africa?
When was Egypt formed? • What was life like in Egypt? • What can be seen of Ancient Egypt?
Who were the Greeks? • How did the Greeks live? • Was Greek culture important?
How big was the Roman Empire? • What was life like in Rome?
What was the impact of Roman rule?

EXPLORERS 60

Who were the first explorers? • How did early explorers find their way?
How far did the Vikings travel? • Who were the first Arab explorers? • Who first made contact
with China? • When was the Great Age of Exploration? • Who discovered America?
Who first sailed around the world? • Who were the "Conquistadors?"
Who found out about Australia? • Who explored Africa?
How were polar regions explored?

PLANET EARTH 84

What is a planet? • What is the earth made of? • How many oceans are there?
How are coastlines shaped? • Have there always been mountains? • How are rivers made?
Are all deserts hot and sandy? • What is a glacier? • Where are the polar regions?
What is climate? • What are the Earth's natural resources? • Are we damaging the planet?

Contents

THE SEA 108

What do we know about the sea? • What is an ocean? • What are currents and tides?
How are waves formed? • What is on the seashore? • What lives in the sea?
What is in the ocean depths? • What is a coral reef? • How do we use the sea?
How do we enjoy the sea? • What sea legends are there?
How do we look after the sea? • What is the sea's future?

THE WEATHER 134

What is weather? • What is air pressure? • What is wind? • What are clouds?
Why do we need rain? • When does it snow? • What causes thunderstorms?
Is weather different at sea? • How strange can weather be? • How are forecasts made?
Can we predict the weather? • Is our climate changing?

SPACE 158

What is space? • What is a galaxy? • What is a solar system? • What is the Sun?
What are planets made of? • Could people live on the Moon? • What is an asteroid belt?
Why do stars twinkle? • How are stars formed? • Who were the first astronomers?
How are spacecraft launched? • Who were the first astronauts?
How can you find out more?

TEST YOUR KNOWLEDGE 184

This section is full of questions with a difference – the answers can only be read when you
hold the book up to a mirror! Use this extra section to quiz yourself and your friends!

INDEX 190

What are dinosaurs?

Diplodocus

An unusual early reptile was Lonisquama which lived in Asia 240 million years ago. Only 6 in. long, its back carried a row of stiff, tall scales.

Dinosaurs lived millions of years ago. They were reptiles, a group of animals that today includes lizards and snakes, turtles and tortoises, crocodiles and alligators.

Q How many different types of dinosaur are there?

A Scientists have grouped dinosaurs into several sorts:

 THERAPODS include all the meat-eating (carnivorous), two-legged dinosaurs like Tyrannosaurus.

 SAUROPODS are giant plant-eating (herbivorous) dinosaurs like Apatosaurus and Diplodocus.

 ORNITHOPODS are smaller, plant-eating dinosaurs which walked on two legs, like Iguanodon and the duck-billed dinosaurs or hadrosaurs, such as Tsintaosaurus.

 CERATOPSIANS include horned dinosaurs like Triceratops, and other plant-eaters.

 STEGOSAURS include dinosaurs armed with plates, like Stegosaurus. They were plant-eaters and walked on four legs.

 ANKYLOSAURS This group includes other armored dinosaurs like Nodosaurus. Like the stegosaurs, they were plant-eaters and walked on four legs.

 PACHYCEPHALOSAURS The name means "thick-headed" and describes a group of dinosaurs with very thick skulls, named after the best-known, Pachycephalosaurus.

Triceratops

Tsintaosaurus

Q When did dinosaurs live?

A Dinosaurs lived only during the Mesozoic Era, or so-called Age of Reptiles. The Mesozoic Era lasted from 225 million to 64 million years ago. No one has ever seen a dinosaur. The earliest of human ancestors did not appear on Earth until four million years ago.

Q Were dinosaurs the first reptiles?

A Many other types of reptile lived before the dinosaurs. The very earliest reptile that scientists have recognized was found in Scotland in 1989 in rocks 335 million years old.

Tanystropheus was a 9.8 ft. long early reptile which lived 250 million years ago. Its neck was incredibly long.

The sprawl of an early reptile (left) and the upright legs of a dinosaur (right).

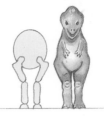

Tyrannosaurus

Stegosaurus

Pachycephalosaurus

Nodosaurus

Q Where did the dinosaurs come from?

A Fossil evidence shows that a group of reptiles living in Argentina about 230 million years ago developed a new way of walking. Instead of walking with sprawling steps like crocodiles, they  began to walk with their legs more directly under their bodies, like the dinosaurs. One reptile called *Lagosuchus* may have been the ancestor of all the dinosaurs.

Q How do you tell the difference between dinosaurs and other fossil reptiles?

A Two important things make a dinosaur. First, they all lived on the land. Second, they all walked on upright legs. All other reptiles, whether fossil or living, had different ways of moving.

Q Did all the dinosaurs live at the same time?

A The dinosaurs lived throughout the Mesozoic Era. Different sorts lived at different times.

Q What was the very first dinosaur?

A What is believed to be the world's oldest dinosaur was found in Argentina in 1991. Named Eoraptor, it lived 228 million years ago. It was over three feet long, perhaps the size of a large dog. Other early dinosaurs have been found in South America and even older ones may still be discovered.

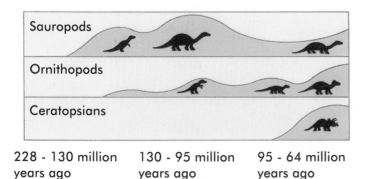

Sauropods		
Ornithopods		
Ceratopsians		
228 - 130 million years ago	130 - 95 million years ago	95 - 64 million years ago

Plateosaurus has been found in western Europe in large groups of skeletons. They probably traveled in herds.

Dinosaur fossils have been found on every continent, even in Antarctica. But since dinosaurs first appeared on Earth, the positions of the continents have changed a great deal.

Plateosaurus

Q Did any dinosaurs live all over the world?

A No single type of dinosaur lived everywhere, but some groups were more common than others. *Plateosaurus* belonged to a small early group called the *prosauropods*. Relatives have been found in the United States, Germany, and South Africa.

Q Where did *Tyrannosaurus* live?

A *Tyrannosaurus rex* is the one dinosaur every one knows. But there are very few examples of skeletons and most are quite incomplete. They were all found in the United States, mainly in Montana.

Q Are dinosaurs found in every country?

A No, but certainly in very many. Famous finds have been made in what is now the United States, South America, Canada, Tanzania, China Mongolia, Australia and India, as well as many European countries.

The continents to-day are still moving. North America and Europe are difting apart from each other about as fast as a fingernail grows.

Pachycephalosaurus and its relatives had skulls up to 10 in. thick on top! Scientists have guessed that head-butting contests were held to defend territory or for rivals to fight over the leadership of a herd.

Q How could the same dinosaurs live on different continents - did they swim across the ocean?

A For many millions of years, they would not have needed to. The continents have been drifting apart slowly ever since they were formed. Today, *Brachiosaurus* can be found in two continents - Africa and North America. When *Brachiosaurus* was alive it was still all one continent.

Q Did dinosaurs have homes?

A The largest dinosaurs may have had favourite resting places on the edges of forests or beneath cliffs. The smaller dinosaurs could perhaps nestle in more sheltered spots safe from their enemies.

Q Did dinosaurs always live in one place?

A Some herbivorous dinosaurs may have migrated in search of fresh grazing.

Q Were dinosaurs in the Antarctic cold?

A The Earth's climate was much warmer during the dinosaur's reign. The continent we now call Antarctica was much nearer to the Equator. The dinosaurs would not have seen any ice-caps! Reptiles cannot survive very cold climates.

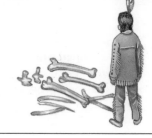

When Gideon Mantell first showed his dinosaur teeth to other scientists of the day, they were identified as being from a rhinoceros!

Early in the nineteenth century, some strange fossils were found in southern England. They were recognized as being from creatures entirely new to science. No one really knew what these creatures looked like.

Q **When were the first dinosaurs found?**

A Gideon Mantell, a doctor from England, found the teeth of *Iguanodon* in 1822. In 1824, William Buckland described some bones which he called *Megalosaurus*, but found some years before. After these discoveries, many people began to hunt for the fossil bones of these new giant lizards.

Q **Why didn't anyone ever find them before?**

A We know that dinosaur bones were found but no one realized that they had once belonged to huge extinct reptiles. One bone was thought to be from a giant man!

Iguanodon got its name because its teeth looked like giant versions of the living marine iguana from the Galapagos.

Q **Why do dinosaurs have such funny names?**

A Each dinosaur is given a special name using words made up from two ancient languages, Latin and Greek. The names usually mean something which describes the creature in some way. *Megalosaurus* means "big lizard." The same dinosaur names are used by all scientists worldwide.

For hundreds of years, the Blackfoot Indians of Canada thought that the dinosaur bones they found were the remains of their ancestors!

Dinosaur teeth have been collected by Chinese doctors for over 2,000 years. They are believed to come from dragons and are ground into powder and used for medicines!

Q What did they think dinosaurs looked like when they first found their bones?

A Gideon Mantell drew the first reconstruction of a dinsaur in 1835. He first thought that *Iguanodon* must have been like a giant lizard some 69 ft. long. In fact, we now know that is about 32 ft. long. In 1854, several life-sized models of dinosaurs were built in the gardens of Crystal Palace, London. *Iguanodon* is still there today, looking rather like a rhinoceros!

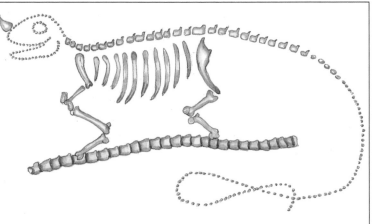

Q When was the first complete skeleton of a dinosaur found?

A The first was also one of the most spectacular finds ever. In 1878, almost forty skeletons of *Iguanodon* were found in a coal mine in Belgium.

Megalosaurus was the first dinosaur to get a scientific name.

Q Who gave dinosaurs their name?

A Dinosaur means "terrible lizard." The name was invented by a famous scientist called Richard Owen in 1842.

Q What was the first dinosaur to be found in North America?

A Huge numbers of dinosaurs have been found in North America. The first was an early *sauropod* called *Anchisaurus*, found near in the state of Conneticut. Some fragments were found in 1818 and were thought to be human! By 1855 it was decided that they must be reptilian.

'Supersaurus' had a shoulder blade 8 ft. long!

When complete skeletons are found, scientists can be fairly sure that they can put the bones together in the right order. But could we guess what you look like just from your skeleton?

Q How do scientists know how to put dinosaur bones together?

A Scientists use their knowledge of other animals to put dinosaur skeletons together. But for a long time after dinosaurs were first discovered, many mistakes were made. *Apatosaurus* even got the wrong head for nearly one hundred years because it was originally found without one!

Q Were dinosaurs fat or thin?

A It is difficult to tell if a dinosaur was fat or thin as fossils are usually just the remains of their hard parts - normally bones and teeth. Modern plant-eaters such as elephants, hippos and cattle, have big stomachs - and plant-eating dinosaurs were probably just as fat. Smaller, more agile dinosaurs needed to be slimmer to move quickly. Scientists and artists have to use comparisons like this to get an idea of how each dinosaur might have looked.

Early this century, some scientists thought that the legs of Diplodocus sprawled like a lizard. But its chest would have dragged along the ground!

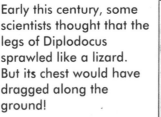

Q What was the smallest dinosaur?

A Perhaps the smallest dinosaur was *Compsognathus*. Fully grown it was only 4 ft. long and most of this was a long tail.

Compsognathus

Mamenchisaurus was 72 ft. long but 33 ft. of that was its neck! It lived in China 160 million years ago.

Gideon Mantell thought that an odd spike-shaped bone he found must be a horn on the nose of Iguanodon. It turned out to be a thumb!

Q What was dinosaur skin like?

A A few fossils of dinosaur skin have been found. It was tough, dry, waterproof and made of small rounded scales. Sometimes there is armor plating.

What was the biggest dinosaur?

The largest complete skeleton known is of *Brachiosaurus* - 39 ft. tall, 75 ft. long and weighing 78 tons. The longest dinosaur known is *Diplodocus*, whose skeleton was up to 88 ft. long. But some new finds from Colorado and New Mexico might be from even bigger dinosaurs. *Supersaurus*, *Ultrasaurus* and the largest *Seismosaurus*, were truly gigantic. *Seismosaurus* would have been similar to *Diplodocus* but may have been over 118 ft. long and weighed up to 145 tons! This would have been the biggest animal ever to have lived.

Diplodocus

Brachiosaurus

Q If no-one has seen a dinosaur, how can scientists be sure that they get dinosaurs to look right?

A We can never be sure what dinosaurs looked like. Scientists still argue about the way many dinosaurs might have appeared. Even well-known dinosaurs like *Iguanodon* can be made to look quite different when drawn in different poses.

Q What color were dinosaurs?

A Even fossils of skin cannot tell us what color it was. Modern reptiles, especially the lizards have a wonderful variety of colors and patterns and dinosaurs may have been just as colorful. Bright patches of color might have been important for the dinosaurs to recognize each other and to display warning signs. The large plant-eating dinosaurs were probably camouflaged. But would we have guessed at the Zebra's stripes with only bones to study?

Euoplocephalus stunned its attackers with the bony club on the end of its tail.

Some dinosaurs ate only plants. Others ate only meat. Plant-eating animals are called herbivores and meat-eating animals are called carnivores.

Some dinosaurs had up to two thousand teeth.

Q Which dinosaurs ate only plants?

A Most dinosaurs ate plants. The huge *sauropods*, the largest of all the dinosaurs, are the best known. They had long bodies, tails and necks, and small heads with special teeth for grazing. With their long necks they could reach up into trees.

Dinosaurs never ate grass. It did not appear on Earth until after the dinosaurs had become extinct.

Diplodocus

Q How can you tell what a dinosaur ate?

A Fossils of the teeth and jaws are the most important clues. Narrow, curved, sharp teeth belong

to the carnivores like *Tyrannosaurus*. Herbivorous dinosaurs have flatter, grinding teeth like *Camarasaurus*, or sharp nipping teeth like *Iguanodon*. *Ceratopsians* had beaks to help tear off leaves.

Q How did dinosaurs protect themselves from attack?

A Many dinosaurs were protected by armor. This included hard plates, horns and spikes.

Stegosaurus

Plant-eating dinosaurs swallowed stones to help grind leaves up in their stomachs.

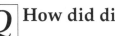

Fossils of dinosaur droppings have helped scientists discover what dinosaurs ate. But which dropping came from which dinosaur?

Q How did dinosaurs kill?

A Carnivorous dinosaurs had sharp claws as well as sharp teeth: both would have made good weapons. Some large carnivores, such as *Tyrannosaurus*, may have used their huge heavy skulls as battering rams.

Q Did dinosaurs eat each other?

A Some carnivores were fast and would have chased other dinosaurs, perhaps even their own kind. They may have hunted in packs like hyaenas. Small *Coelophysis* skeletons were found in an adult *Coelophysis*. Large carnivores, like *Tyrannosaurus*, were too heavy to chase prey and perhaps fed off dead or slower moving dinosaurs.

Tyrannosaurus teeth were more than 6 in. long and very sharp for slicing and tearing at flesh.

No one knows what Tyrannosaurus used its very short arms for as they did not even reach its mouth!

Tyrannosaurus measured 45 ft. in length and stood almost 20 ft. high.

Q How much did dinosaurs eat?
A Plant-eating dinosaurs ate most of the time to get enough nourishment. Diplodocus ate about a ton of leaves a day! The meat-eating dinosaurs' diet was much richer so they did not need to eat huge quantities regularly.

Q What else was there for dinosaurs to eat?
A Small reptiles, birds, fish and insects were all food for the dinosaurs.

Could dinosaurs run?

The arrangement of the bones in the ankles and feet of dinosaurs show that all except the *sauropods* and *stegosaurs* could run, and footprints prove that they did!

Dryosaurus

Ceratosaurus

Q How fast could dinosaurs run?

A A trackway made by *Tyrannosaurus* shows that it could have outrun a charging rhinoceros, perhaps reaching 30 miles per hour. The fastest of all was a small two-footed dinosaur which left footprints showing that it could run at nearly 45 miles per hour: but we don't know which dinosaur it was! The great sauropod dinosaurs like *Apatosaurus* walked at a speed of only 3 - 5 miles per hour.

Q Did dinosaurs leave any other marks but footprints?

A In only very rare cases, marks have been found where dinosaur tails dragged along the ground. Generally though, despite the enormous size of some tails, they were held up above the ground, and not just when running.

Just as lions hunt zebras today, the meat-eating dinosaurs hunted the plant-eaters. The carnivores ran to catch - the herbivores ran to escape.

Q Could dinosaurs hop, skip or jump?

A Once, some footprints were believed to have been made by a hopping dinosaur but are now thought to have been made by a turtle swimming in shallow water. Footprints have been found showing a dinosaur with a missing toe, and another with a limp! Scientists believe that at least the active *therapods* could jump, but there is no evidence from footprints! Ninety-nine out of a hundred trackways show walking dinosaurs.

Fossil footprints give us clues about the shape of the foot as well as the weight and speed of the dinosaur. There are sometimes skin impressions too.

Though many dinosaurs could run well, they may not have been able to run for long distances before becoming exhausted.

Q Where are fossil footprints found?

A Throughout the world there are about a thousand places where dinosaur tracks have been found. One of the most famous is at the Davenport Ranch in Texas, in rocks one hundred million years old. There, and in nearby places, thousands of footprints have been found.

Q Are there any footprints of young dinosaurs?

A One of the Texas trackways contains the footprints left by twenty-three *sauropod* dinosaurs which seem to have been traveling as a herd. Many of them are quite small, probably youngsters. The larger members of the herd traveled in front and at the sides of the herd, the smaller ones were protected in the center.

Q How can footprints be fossilized?

A Dinosaurs crossing muddy lake or seashores leave behind their footprints, just as animals do today. If the mud dries in the hot sun, the next tide or flood washes more mud into the imprints which are then preserved.

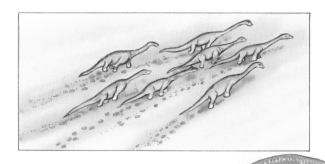

Lesothosaurus

Q Which dinosaurs could run the fastest?

A The dinosaurs which could run the fastest had two long hind legs, and were small and slim. *Hypsilophodon* from England and *Lesothosaurus* from southern Africa were both herbivores that could run fast.

Could dinosaurs swim?

Plesiosaurs have long necks, short bodies and large paddle-like limbs, rather like modern sea lions.

Like any land-living animals today - elephants, hippopotamuses and buffaloes - dinosaurs enjoyed a good paddle and swim.

Q Were any dinosaurs amphibious?

A This was an old idea. It was once thought that the heaviest dinosaurs like *Brachiosaurus* and *Apatosaurus* were too large to support their own weight on land, and therefore had to live in water. Scientists have now calculated that their large leg bones were strong enough to support them out of the water.

Q If the Loch Ness monster really does exist, wouldn't it be a swimming dinosaur?

A If Nessie ever was found and proved to be a reptile, she would almost certainly turn out to be a *plesiosaur*, *ichthyosaur* or *pliosaur*. These were all marine reptiles and were not dinosaurs, which only lived on land.

Q Did any dinosaurs live permanently in the water?

A Probably not but ideas change. The long necks of dinosaurs like *Mamenchisaurus* were once thought to be useful for breathing in deep water. Unfortunately, water pressure at those depths - 32 ft. or more - would not have allowed the lungs to work.

Apatosaurus being chased by Allosaurus

Ichthyosaurs looked rather like modern sharks and dolphins.

Many modern creatures like dogs, elephants, polar bears and even cows can swim. They don't need flippers or webbed feet and dinosaurs may have been able to swim just as well.

Q Did the swimming reptiles live at the same time as the dinosaurs?

A Throughout the reign of the dinosaurs, the *ichthyosaurs* and *plesiosaurs* were very common in the seas and oceans of the world. There were many types, including the *pliosaurs* and *elasmosaurs*. The largest of all was an Australian *pliosaur* called *Kronosaurus* which grew as large as 42.6 feet.

Q Could dinosaurs float?

A Despite the enormous size of some, there is no reason to suppose that any dinosaur would sink. One set of *Brontosaur* footprints shows only impressions from the front feet! It seems that the dinosaur was floating in a lake and simply kicked itself along with its front feet.

Q Could dinosaurs have fed under water?

A Perhaps, for water plants would be good food. Dinosaurs with weak teeth like the *ankylosaurs* may have grazed rather like hippos or like ducks in shallow water. The long hollow crest of *Parasaurolophus* was once thought to be a sort of snorkel used while feeding below the water.

Q Did any dinosaurs have flippers to help them swim?

A There may be one dinosaur that did. One species of *Compsognathus* found in Germany seems to have had flipper-like front legs. No one is sure, but perhaps they allowed it to swim extra quickly to catch prey or escape from its own hunters.

Longisquama glided through the air with its long scaly wings.

Some small dinosaurs have skeletons almost identical to *Archaeopteryx* - the oldest known bird. The dinosaur ancestors of the birds must have developed the ability to fly or glide short distances.

Q How well could *Archaeopteryx* fly?

A Probably not very well. Compared to modern birds its muscles were weak and it was much heavier. But it could have flapped its wings quite well and its bony, feathered tail would have made a good rudder to help it maneuver on long glides through the air.

Q How did dinosaurs get feathers?

A Reptile scales like those on snakes and lizards may have become feathery to help keep the smaller dinosaurs warm. Only later did they also prove useful for flying.

Q How did the dinosaurs learn to fly?

A Perhaps like many living animals (including frogs, squirrels and monkeys), small, feathered dinosaurs began to jump, glide and parachute from tree to tree, chasing prey or escaping from danger.

Archaeopteryx was discovered in Germany in rocks 150 million years old. Alongside its fossil bones are clear impressions of feathers forming two wings and a tail.

The Dodo lived on the island of Mauritius in the Indian Ocean. Because it could not fly it was easily hunted and became extinct by the end of the sixteenth century.

Q How could giants like dinosaurs have flown?

A *Tyrannosaurus* would never have got airborne! Some carnivorous dinosaurs though, like *Compsognathus* and *Ornitholestes*, were very small, lightly built with hollow bones and could run quickly. Perhaps they chased small lizards and insects and began to take to the air.

Q Are there any other fossil birds?

A Fossils of birds are very rare: their light hollow bones do not fossilize well. Examples that have been found include birds similar to large terns, ostriches, eagles and the Dodo.

Q Isn't a *Pteranodon* a flying dinosaur?

A No. Although they lived on Earth at the same time as the dinosaurs, *Pteranodons* belong to a group of flying reptiles, called *pterosaurs*.

Pteranodon

Q How did *pterosaurs* learn to fly before the dinosaurs?

A The skeletons of the earliest known flying reptiles are similar to ancient carnivorous reptiles alive before the dinosaurs. Their skeletons were light and perhaps they too, like the later feathered dinosaurs climbed trees and learned to glide.

When dinosaur eggs are found, it is not always possible to say which dinosaur laid them.

Did dinosaurs have babies?

All living creatures reproduce and dinosaurs were no exception. It is believed that, like almost all living reptiles, dinosaurs laid eggs.

Q Have any fossil dinosaur eggs ever been found?

A Yes. The first ones found were discovered in the Gobi Desert of Mongolia in 1921. They were neatly arranged in nests and were discovered with skeletons of the small horned dinosaur, *Protoceratops*.

Q Did all dinosaurs lay eggs?

A Fossil eggs have been found with *sauropods, ceratopsians* and a variety of other dinosaurs. However, they are very rare and the majority of dinosaurs have left no fossil eggs. But most scientists assume that all dinosaurs did lay eggs.

Q What do dinosaur eggs look like?

A Unlike most modern reptiles, dinosaurs seem to have laid eggs with hard shells. Eggs that have been found whole are usually oval shaped, blunt at one end with a wrinkled surface. In the case of *Protoceratops*, they were about 8 in. long and laid in nests up to thirty or more at a time. Other eggs are usually between 4.5 and 6.5 inches long (as big as an ostrich egg).

A mother Maiasaura with her babies.

Eggs of the dinosaurs Orodemus and Troodon have been x-rayed and contain the tiny fossilized bones of embryos.

Some fossils of Chasmosaurus show that in herds, they formed a protective circle around their young to guard them from attack.

A herd of Chasmosaurus

Q Were dinosaurs good parents?

A Even the fiercest alligator living today is a very caring parent, feeding and protecting its tiny young. The remains of *Maiasaura* dinochicks were found in Montana. Though their teeth show wear from eating, they were still in their nests. They must have been fed by their parents until they grew old enough to leave home.

Q How did young dinosaurs tell their mothers from their fathers?

A Scientists can only guess whether a fossilized dinosaur is male or female. In a few examples where many skeletons have been found together, some are bigger than others - perhaps the males. We can be sure that baby dinosaurs knew the difference!

Q Are there any fossils of baby dinosaurs?

A The smallest dinosaur skeleton is only 8 in. long - about the size of a blackbird. It has been called *Mussaurus* (mouse-lizard) but it is in fact a very young dinochick of a yet-unknown dinosaur. Other dinosaur babies found include *Protoceratops*, *Maiasaura*, *Psittacosaurus* and *Coelophysis*.

Baby Maiasaura

Q Did the gigantic *sauropods* lay gigantic eggs?

A The largest eggs found weighed 15 lbs. in weight - not much compared to 22 ton sauropods!

Is this what Stenonychosaurus might have looked like if it had continued evolving?

Were dinosaurs stupid?

The original discoverers of *Apatosaurus* and *Diplodocus* were surprised at the small size of the heads compared to the bodies of the dinosaurs. They thought that with such tiny brains, the dinosaurs must have had little intelligence. To-day, we are not so sure.

Q Which was the cleverest dinosaur?

A Size for size, *Stenonychosaurus* must have been the brightest dinosaur. Its brain is similar in proportion to birds and even some mammals, and much bigger than crocodiles.

Q Does a large brain mean that a dinosaur was clever?

A Brains control behaviour and the senses, as well as cleverness. The small carnivorous dinosaurs had large brains compared to the size of their bodies. As a result they had excellent vision, could move quickly and were good at learning how to hunt and catch their prey.

Stenonychosaurus

The brain of the Chinese stegosaur Tuojiangosaurus weighed only about 2.5 ounces.

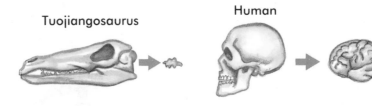

Tuojiangosaurus

Human

Q How big were dinosaur brains?

A For reptiles, most dinosaurs seem to have had quite large brains. The smaller, faster carnivores had the largest brains, though the largest of all was perhaps *Tyrannosaurus*. The *stegosaurs* had perhaps the smallest brains - about the size of a walnut!

Q How do you measure the brain of a dinosaur?

A Sometimes, when mud and sand surrounded a dinosaur skull after death, it filled the brain cavity too. The result - a fossil brain! Different areas of the brain can be seen as well as the bony passages for nerves and blood vessels.

Tuojiangosaurus

Q Which dinosaurs were the most stupid?

A The *sauropods* score lowest in the brain stakes. But however small their brains were, they were obviously good enough for them to survive as a group for 150 million years.

Q Did the enormous *sauropods* have enormous brains?

A Not necessarily so. Brains do not automatically get bigger in proportion to bodies. It depends what dinosaurs did. The more active the dinosaur, the larger the brain needed to be to produce quicker reactions.

Q Do living reptiles have large brains?

A On average, crocodile and alligator brains are approximately the same size as similar sized dinosaurs. The brains of living mammals are ten times the size of similar sized living reptiles.

Crocodile

Some scientists believe that sauropod dinosaurs like Barosaurus might have had up to 8 hearts to help pump blood up their long necks.

How did their bodies work?

A Barosaur heart

The flesh and organs of all creatures rot away after death. To understand how the bodies of dinosaurs worked, scientists have to build up their ideas on very little evidence.

Q What did dinosaur blood look like?

A Like modern animals, dinosaurs needed blood to carry oxygen, heat and food around their bodies. Their blood was probably much the same as our own. To pump this blood, the dinosaurs needed hearts. Those of the biggest dinosaurs must have been enormous to pump blood to heads as high as 82 feet above the ground.

Q What was a dinosaur's normal body temperature?

A We will never know for sure. Reptiles today keep their bodies warm by sun bathing. This can limit their movement in cold weather, so most reptiles live in warm climates. Mammals and birds rely on their own bodies to release heat from food. If they were as active as we think they were, dinosaurs may have been able to do the same thing. Once the biggest dinosaurs were warm, they would probably never have cooled down!

Barosaurus

Q Does fossil bone have fossil blood in it?

A Blood unfortunately does not fossilize, but some bony passages for blood vessels do. Microscopic studies of dinosaur bone have shown that it resembles the bone of living warm-blooded mammals, rather than the so-called cold-blooded living reptiles. This means that the dinosaurs may have been much more active than their living relatives.

Q How do we know what muscles dinosaurs had?

A Muscles are attached to bones. Because of this, bones carry scars of where the muscles were once fixed. The size and position of these marks on dinosaur bones allow scientists to reconstruct the shapes of legs, arms, hips and shoulders. Living reptiles also give some good clues.

Ouranosaurus had long spines running down its backbone. These would have been covered with skin to form a "sail." It could warm up and cool down by directing its sail toward or away from the sun.

Gallimimus had very large eyes. Each eye was supported in its socket by a ring of bony plates which are often fossilized.

Ouranosaurus

The nostrils of the duck-bill dinosaur called Saurolophus are thought to have been covered by an inflatable pouch of skin. Perhaps like many birds, Saurolophus could blow this up into a large, colorful baloon to warn off rivals or to signal to the opposite sex.

Q How big were dinosaur ears?

A There is no evidence that any dinosaur had outer ears like elephants or even ourselves. Like modern reptiles and birds, dinosaur ears would probably have been visible on the surface of their heads. They would look like circular marks in the skin.

Q What color were dinosaurs' eyes?

A We will never know the answer, but the eyes of living reptiles are usually bright and yellow. They are not surrounded by white like our own. Scientists can tell from dinosaur skulls that most had large eyes and so could probably see very well.

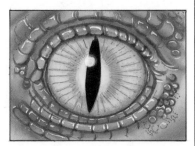

Q How did dinosaurs smell?

A Dinosaurs had holes in their skulls for the nostrils to allow for breathing. They probably used them for smelling too. Some dinosaurs like *Camarasaurus* had very large nostrils on top of the head. Scientists once thought that these helped the dinosaurs to breathe underwater.

Some scientists believe that less than ten percent of dinosaur types that ever existed have been found fossilized.

How do you find a dinosaur?

Fossils are found in rocks formed from mud and sand left by water or wind. They are called sedimentary rocks. Identifying the right rocks of the right age is a good start to finding dinosaurs.

Q How do dinosaurs turn into fossils?

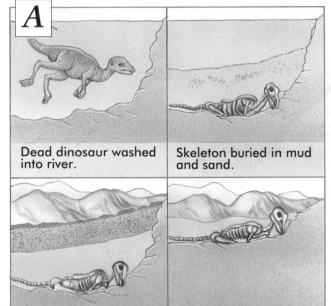

Dead dinosaur washed into river.

Skeleton buried in mud and sand.

Mud and sand turn into rock, bones into fossils.

Millions of years later erosion reveals the fossils.

Q How do they know if the rocks are old enough to contain dinosaur fossils?

A All sorts of plants and animals lived with the dinosaurs and their fossils are much more common: ferns, snails, freshwater fish, shellfish and even insects. Recognizing the right type of rocks with the right type of fossils shows that dinosaurs might be around.

Q How do scientists know where to look for a dinosaur?

A The most common fossils are found in rocks formed under water, especially the seas or oceans. Dinosaurs only lived on the land and so are not so common. They are found in rocks that formed near rivers, lakes, seashores and also deserts.

Q Where do you start to dig?

A Fossils are usually found where the rocks can be seen - quarries, cliffs, or mountains. Fossil hunters then hunt for odd bones sticking out of the rock, made visible by wind and rain. *Baryonyx* was discovered by a man who found only a single claw in a busy quarry. Most of the skeleton was found later by expert excavation.

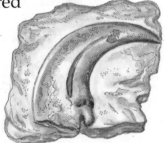

Some of the dinosaur fossils found early this century have still not been fully extracted from the rock in which they were collected.

Before dinosaur bones are removed from an excavation, they are coccooned in plaster of Paris or foam jackets to protect them, especially for long journeys back to the laboratory.

Q How do you dig up a dinosaur?

A Excavating a dinosaur is not an easy job! After discovery, several tons of rock might need to be moved by diggers, bulldozers and pneumatic drills. Hammers and chisels might be used for more careful work before a bone can be removed.

Q What do you do with a dinosaur once it has been dug up?

A Bones may be cracked and only partly visible in their enclosing rock. They are taken to laboratories where the rock is carefully removed with special tools and cracks are constantly repaired. It may be years before all the bones are prepared. Only if the bones are in very good condition might they be joined to make a skeleton.

Q Are there any dinosaurs left to find?

A Though it is very rare to find a completely new dinosaur, *Baryonyx* is a dinosaur unlike any other, and it was found in 1982. In Canada, millions of dinosaur bones can be seen scattered in Dinosaur Provincial Park: three or four complete skeletons are found each year.

Dinosaur skeletons in museums are often plaster casts molded from the real bones. Dinosaurs are too precious to risk damage.

Diplodocus skeleton

Because dinosaur skeletons are rarely complete, model bones are often added to the real skeleton to make up for any that are missing.

You can collect dinosaur models, toys, games and even postage stamps from around the world.

The study of fossils is called palaeontology ("old-life study"). Many years of education are needed to become a paleontologist, but there are lots of ways to become interested in dinosaurs.

Make a catalogue in a notebook to help you remember what the fossils are and what you know about them.

Q What do you have to study at school to become a dinosaur expert?

A All fossils are the remains of once living creatures so biology is important. Mathematics and English will always be useful and later, physics and chemistry.

Q Can you learn about dinosaurs in college?

A There are no courses especially about dinosaurs. In college you learn about different aspects of geology - rocks, minerals and fossils, and the processes that have made and shaped the Earth. You could also study zoology and learn about living animals before specializing in dinosaur studies.

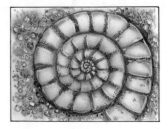

Q How can I find dinosaur fossils?

A It helps if you live in an area where dinosaur fossils are known to occur - but you would still have to be very lucky. The most common dinosaur finds are probably teeth. Start by making a collection of other fossils to get some experience. Leaflets and books may be found in libraries, shops and museums.

The first dinosaur skeleton to be put together was an Iguanodon from Belgium. It was assembled in 1882. The bones were hung from scaffolding by ropes so that they could be moved until they looked right. Then they were supported by an iron frame.

Q What do I need to look for fossils?

A A hammer and chisel are useful to split open rocks. Protective clothing is needed too - gloves for hammering, goggles to guard your eyes and a hard hat to protect your head, especially near cliffs.

Model-makers and artists must work closely with paleontologists if their models and pictures are to look right. Muscles are carefully drawn onto a skeleton outline and the skin added so that the basic shape is right.

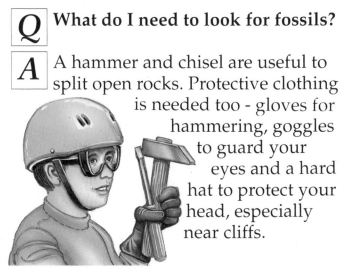

Triceratops

Q What do I do if I find a fossil?

A Remove the fossil carefully and wrap in paper towels or tissues. Make a note of where and when you found it. At home, clean away loose dirt with a dry brush. If this does not work, try brushing with a little water. When the fossil is dry write a number on it for use in a catalogue of your finds. Store your fossil safely by making a tissue 'nest' for it in a box or drawer.

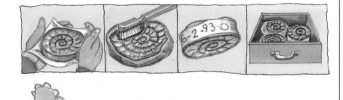

Q What tips are there for collecting fossils?

A Never collect without the permission of the landowner.

Never collect from cliffs or quarry walls. It is much safer to work on fallen blocks or waste tips.

Do not be greedy - leave some fossils for others to find.

Replace your poorer fossils when you find better examples.

Q Can I get any help?

A Visit your local museum and ask if there is a geologist on the staff. If you have collected fossils, someone may help you to identify them. You may also be able to find out if there is a local geological society. Society members will include many enthusiastic collectors. Find out from them about the latest information on dinosaurs.

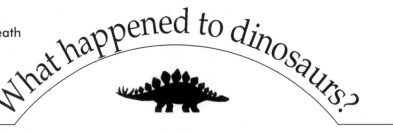

A popular theory for the death of the dinosaurs is that a six mile-wide meterorite, traveling at 60,000 mph, hit the Earth.

There are no dinosaurs alive today. One of the great mysteries in the history of life on Earth is why such a successful group of animals should become extinct.

Q When did the dinosaurs become extinct?

A Rocks about seventy million years old, from all over the world contain dinosaur fossils. Amazingly, only five or six million years later, not a single dinosaur had survived.

Q What was the last type of dinosaur to live?

A It is not always easy to tell whether rocks in one place on Earth are a little bit younger or older than rocks in other places. So, we are not sure if some dinosaurs outlived others thousands of miles away. Certainly the last dinosaur groups included *Tyrannosaurus*, *Triceratops* and *Parasaurolophus*. A bone-head dinosaur (*pachycephalosaur*) called *Stygimoloch* from Montana, may have been the very last to survive - but only a few pieces of broken skull have been found.

Q What could have caused the dinosaurs to die out?

A Possible explanations for dinosaur extinction:

Funny	Mistakes	Serious
Boredom - after 150 million years.	Constipation from the new flowering plants.	Competition from the mammals.
Only male or female dinosaurs left.	Eggs eaten by the mammals.	Climate getting colder.
Too much smoking.	Disease from a new virus.	Brains got smaller.
New caterpillars ate all the leaves.	Holes in the ozone layer caused by radiation.	High temperatures caused by a meteorite explosion.

Q What else became extinct with the dinosaurs?

A All the large marine reptiles - the *mosasaurs* and *plesiosaurs*, as well as the flying reptiles, disappeared. Also some types of shellfish, including the *ammonites* and *belemnites*, and huge numbers of microscopic marine plants vanished.

Ammonite

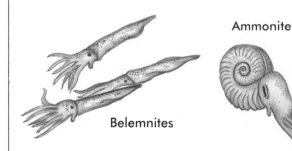

Belemnites

Iridium, a common element in meterorites, has been found worldwide in rocks of the same age.

In Mexico, fossil tree trunks have been found mixed up with rocks from the ocean floor. These are evidence of the huge tidal waves that a large meteorite would cause.

Q What survived the great extinction?

A The majority of plants and animals survived. These included the other reptiles such as snakes, lizards, crocodiles and turtles. Birds and the early mammals survived too, together with shellfish, corals, starfish, insects and land plants.

Map of Mexico showing likely area of meteorite impact.

Mexico

Q What do scientists think is the real reason dinosaurs died out?

A Most scientists now agree that two things caused the death of the dinosaurs and many other creatures. First the climate had been gradually cooling down. Second, around 64 million years ago something catastrophic happened. Some people believe a huge meteriorite struck the Earth.

Q How could a meteorite do so much damage?

A A large meteorite hitting the Earth would throw up a gigantic cloud of dust. This would cut out sunlight for months, perhaps years, causing plants and animals to die. Some, like the dinosaurs, never recovered.

Q Is it possible that dinosaurs are alive somewhere on Earth?

A Sadly, though there are occasional stories and legends, no one seriously believes that even a small dinosaur could have remained undetected. But dinosaur descendents are still all around us: the birds.

Under Babylonian law, a son who hit his father had his hands chopped off.

The oldest known civilizations began in the area we now call the Middle East. Some cities, such as Damascus and Jericho, are at least 5,000 years old.

Q How big were the earliest cities?

A The earliest cities were nowhere near as large as modern cities. Çatal Hüyük, in what is now Turkey, was built about 9,000 years ago and had a population of only 5,000. The houses were made of mud bricks and were built up against each other, so there were no streets. People got in and out of their houses through holes in the roof using ladders.

Q What did the Sumerians invent?

A The Sumerians knew how to weave cloth, make things out of metal and make pots on a wheel. But the most important progress they made was in writing, mathematics and astronomy. Their discoveries in these areas enabled them to keep records of taxes and agreements, write down laws and work out a calendar.

Q Where was Mesopotamia?

A Mesopotamia means "the land between the rivers." The area was in what is now Iraq. The rivers were the Tigris and the Euphrates, and the first city dwellers there were known as Sumerians. By 3000 B.C. there were powerful city states, such as Ur and Uruk, which traded with and fought against each other. The cities had populations of up to 50,000 people and were often built around mud-brick temples called ziggurats.

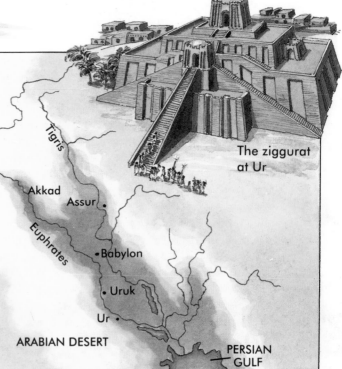

The ziggurat at Ur

Tigris

Akkad

Assur

Euphrates

Babylon

Uruk

Ur

ARABIAN DESERT

PERSIAN GULF

The oldest known set of false teeth belonged to a Phoenician man of 1000 B.C. He had four of someone else's teeth tied to his own with gold wire.

Sargon of Akkad

Q **Which were the most powerful city states?**

A Sargon of Akkad (2370 B.C.) was the first great conqueror that we know about. The Hittites created an empire based around Anatolia between 1800 B.C. and 1200 B.C. The Assyrians were a war-like people from the city state of Assur. They built a huge empire stretching from the Persian Gulf to Egypt, between 800 B.C. and 650 B.C.

Q **What was their writing like?**

A The first writing was pictographic. This means that instead of using letters and words, the Sumerians drew pictures. Later, these pictures came to represent sounds rather than actual objects. Sumerian writing is called "cuneiform," which means "wedge-shaped," because they used a sharp wedge to make marks in the clay tablets on which they wrote.

Cuneiform writing

Q **Where did civilization begin in in the Mediterranean?**

A The Minoan people began to build palaces on the island of Crete around 2200 B.C. The Palace of Knossos could hold up to 80,000 people. Around 1400 B.C. the Minoans were conquered by the Mycenaeans from mainland Greece.

Where is the Indus Valley?

Chess was invented in ancient India as a war game.

The Indus Valley stretches from Tibet, through Pakistan, to the Indian Ocean. The River Indus flows through this valley. Many ancient towns have been discovered there.

Q What was life like in the Indus Valley?

A Two major cities, called Mohenjo Daro and Harappa, have been found in this area, along with the sites of over one hundred other towns. From these ruins scientists have been able to discover many things about this ancient civilization. However, archaeologists have not been able to read the type of writing used by the Indus people at this time, so we still know very little about the way they lived.

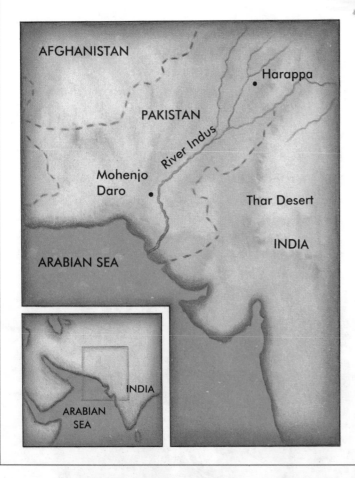

Q How long ago did these cities exist?

A They were probably built around 2500 B.C. and later abandoned around 1500 B.C. Each one was nearly 3 miles in circumference. No one is quite sure why these cities were abandoned, but the most likely explanation is that the Indus River changed course, moving away from the cities.

Q Why were cities built in this area?

A The people of the Indus Valley relied on the annual flooding of the river to provide the mineral-rich silt that made the farmland fertile. Owing to this, all the major towns and cities were built close to the river.

Merchants in Mohenjo Daro used to stamp their goods with seals. Nobody is sure if different merchants used different pictures on their seals, but there have been many different sorts found.

Q Was life in Mohenjo Daro well organized?

A The city was laid out on a rigid street plan and had the world's first known sewer system with drains and manholes. There were wide streets and large granaries for storing food in case the harvest failed. Houses were made out of bricks that were the same size, rather than oddly-shaped pieces of stone. Each house also had its own bathroom and toilet.

Q How did people dress?

A The Indus Valley people were the first in the world to grow cotton and make it into cloth. They also used copper to make jewelery. Men made razors out of copper.

Q What sort of transport did people use?

A Two-wheeled ox carts carried heavy loads over land, and boats were used to transport things up and down the river. Camels and pack horses were used to carry merchants' goods over long distances.

Q What did people do in their spare time?

A They kept pets such as dogs, cats, monkeys, caged birds and insects. Children played with whistles and toys, like pottery monkeys, which danced on pieces of string. Adults played dice games.

What is a dynasty?

荷葉飯

China has the oldest continuous civilization in the world. The country was ruled by different royal families known as dynasties. Little is known about the earliest part of Chinese history.

Q Where did civilization begin in China?

A The first powerful kingdom we know about was based near the fertile Yellow River around 1500 B.C. and was ruled by the Shang Dynasty. In 1027 B.C. the Shang were driven out by the Zhou, who ruled for 800 years.

Q What is the Great Wall of China?

A The Great Wall is the longest wall in the world. It is 2,150 miles long, stretching from the coast to the Gobi Desert. It was meant to keep out invaders from the north, but didn't always do so. The wall was built between 221 B.C. and 206 B.C., and strengthened by later emperors. Most of the present wall was rebuilt during the Ming Period (1368-1644).

Q Who was the first Emperor of the whole of China?

A In 221 B.C. the cruel and ruthless Qin ruler, Cheng, began to call himself Emperor of China. The Qin had overthrown the Zhou in 225 B.C. and ruled the biggest empire seen in history up to that time. Cheng also built the Great Wall of China.

Q Why was silk important?

A Silk was China's main export, sent right across Asia, and even as far as Rome, along trading routes that became known as the "Silk Route." The silk came from the cocoons of silkworms and made a light, soft, strong thread. The Chinese learned how to rear silkworms, feeding them on mulberry leaves. They kept the secret of how to make silk to themselves until 550 A.D., when two Persian monks smuggled silkworms out of China in a hollow cane.

Q What did the Chinese invent?

A The Chinese discovered many different things, including how to make paper and porcelain, a kind of fine pottery. They also discovered that the resin of the lacquer tree could be used to coat wooden bowls so they could hold hot foods and liquids, such as soup. Wheelbarrows were in use a thousand years before they became common in Europe.

Q Who was Confucius ?

A Confucius was a scholar whose ideas about government were influential in China, as well as in other countries. He thought that peace and order were the greatest blessings a country could have. He believed that a ruler should be just and kind and his subjects should be loyal and obedient. Confucius also taught the importance of good manners and self-control.

Q What advances did the Chinese make in science?

A Wang Chong, who lived in the first century A.D., showed that eclipses and the movements of the stars and the moon could be predicted. Zhang Heng made the world's first seismograph, used to detect and record earthquakes. The Chinese also invented a kind of medicine, called acupuncture, which cures people by sticking needles in them.

Pictured is a seismograph. Balls dropped into the frogs' mouths when an earthquake occurred. The more balls that fell, the stronger the earthquake.

38

The Olmecs carved large stone heads which were up to 8.8 feet high.

People migrated from Asia to the American mainland about 30,000 years ago. Sea levels were lower then, and North America was joined to Russia by a land bridge. The first advanced civilizations grew up in Central America.

Q Which were the first important civilizations that we know of?

A The Olmecs lived along the eastern coast of what is now Mexico. Their civilization flourished between 1150 B.C. and 800 B.C. Their sculptures and pottery influenced later cultures. The Maya, from what is now Guatemala, were also important. They flourished between 300 B.C. and 900 A.D.

Q How advanced were they?

A The people of Central America knew about farming, pottery and writing and how to make things out of gold, copper and jade. They also made paper from the bark of wild fig trees. However, they had no knowledge of such things as iron, glass, coins, or the plough.

Q What did the people of Central America eat?

A The basic diet was made up of maize, beans, tomatoes, chili peppers and turkeys. People also reared dogs and guinea pigs to eat.

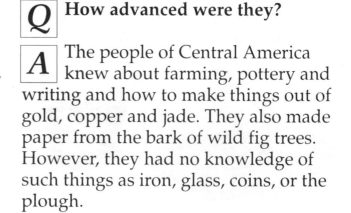

Q What did they use instead of iron?

A For making weapons and cutting tools they used obsidian, a kind of volcanic glass. When it is polished, obsidian has a very sharp edge, though it does break easily.

The Mayas used melted rubber to make waterproof clothing.

Chocolate was first brought to Europe from Central America, where it was made with chilli peppers.

Q **Did they know about the wheel?**

A They knew about the wheel but only used it on toys and not for transport. This was probably because they had no animal strong enough to pull a cart.

Q **What was their religion like?**

A They worshipped gods who represented the Sun, Moon, rain and maize. Human sacrifice was common and caused many wars as city states wanted to capture prisoners to sacrifice.

Q **Can any of the cities still be seen?**

A About forty cities have been discovered so far. The most important buildings were stepped pyramids, used for religious ceremonies. Teotihuacan (which means "Where Men become Gods"), near modern Mexico City, had a population of 200,000 and covered 7.7 sq. mi. The main street was 1.2 mi. long and 130 ft. wide, with over a hundred temples along its sides. The largest building, the Pyramid of the Sun, was over 230 feet high.

Q **Did they play games?**

A We know that they played a game which involved hitting a hard rubber ball at stone markers along the sides of a walled court. Heads, elbows, knees and shoulders could be used to hit the ball, but you could not use hands or feet. During festivals games were played in honor of the gods, and the loser became a human sacrifice.

AFRICA
Tanzania

Were there cities in Africa?

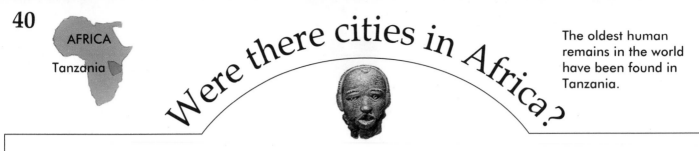

The oldest human remains in the world have been found in Tanzania.

Ancient Africa's greatest civilization developed in Egypt. But there were other important states along its northern coast and in what are now the present-day countries of Sudan and Ethiopia.

Q Did people ever live in the Sahara?

A The Sahara has not always been a desert, and people used to live there until 2000 B.C. Historians know they herded cattle, made pottery, and used four-wheeled vehicles, either as war chariots or as carts for transport.

Q What happened after the Sahara had become a desert?

A The Sahara started to dry up around 10,000 B.C. Some people still managed to live in oases where there was enough water for date palms and their livestock. By using camels, which could go without water for days, traders were able to cross 186 miles of desert in a week. They bought salt and cloth from the north in exchange for slaves, gold and leather from the south.

Q What was Carthage?

A Carthage was originally a colony, founded near present-day Tunis, by the Phoenicians. They were a trading people who lived in what is now Lebanon. In their language it was called Kart-Hadasht, which means "New Town." Carthage grew rich and powerful through trade and its silver mines.

Q What happened to Carthage?

A The Romans feared the growing power of Carthage, and fought three great wars over a hundred years. The Romans were finally victorious in 146 B.C. They totally destroyed Carthage and ploughed up the land where it had once stood.

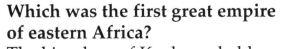

Q Which was the first great empire of eastern Africa?

A The kingdom of Kush, probably founded by people from Egypt, rose on the banks of the Nile River. The kings of Kush were buried in pyramids, like Egyptian pharaohs. The first capital of Kush was founded at Napata, on a bend of the Nile. The kingdom grew rich on the gold it traded with Egypt. After Napata was attacked, the capital was moved to Meroe on the other bank of the Nile.

Q What happened to Kush?

A Kush was a great kingdom for a thousand years. There is evidence of iron production and a high level of trading along the Nile. There were also great palaces and a temple to the Egyptian god, Amon. However, the Kush were overthrown by their neighbor, Aksum, around 300 A.D.

Q How did the kingdom of Aksum grow?

A Aksum was probably founded by a mixture of African and southern Arabian peoples. The capital, also called Aksum, was in the highlands, and there was an important port, called Adulis, which was a major trading point. From 300 B.C. to A.D. 600. Aksum grew rich on the ivory trade.

Q What can be seen of Aksum today?

A Aksum lies in what is now Ethiopia. The ruins of Aksum include a palace with twenty-seven carved thrones. There are also 126 granite columns, some over 98 feet high. Other columns are carved with pictures of multistory houses.

Q Did the Ancient Africans use iron?

A People living around Nok in Nigeria were making iron tools and weapons by about 5000 B.C. By A.D. 400 the use of iron had spread all the way down to southern Africa.

When was Egypt formed?

Pharaoh Ramesses II reigned for sixty-seven years and had over one hundred children.

Lower Egypt, the area around the Nile delta, and Upper Egypt were united under one ruler around 3100 B.C. The Egyptian civilization lasted until 30 B.C., when Egypt became part of the Roman Empire.

Q Why was the ruler called pharaoh?

A The Egyptians thought that their ruler was descended from the Sun god and it would not be respectful for an ordinary person to use his name. They referred to him as pharaoh, or "per a' o" as the Egyptians called him, which means "The Great House."

Q What did the Egyptians call their country?

A The Egyptians called their country "Kmt," which means "The Black Land." This refers to the rich soil along the riverbanks. The desert on either side of the Nile which protected Egypt from invasion by enemies and provided gold and gem stones was called "Dsrt," which means "The Red Land."

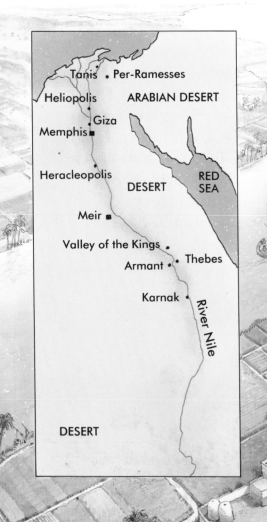

Q Where was the capital?

A The site of the capital changed at different times. The first was at Memphis, midway between Upper and Lower Egypt. During the Middle Kingdom the capital city was further south at Itj-towy. The New Kingdom pharaohs made Thebes the capital and a great religious center. The later capitals of Per-Ramesses and Tanis were in the Nile delta.

The Egyptians were the first people to have bathrooms.

The Egyptians made sticky bandages out of linen coated with honey.

Q When was Egyptian civilization at its height?

A Egypt was at its greatest during periods which historians call the Old Kingdom (2575-2134 B.C.), the Middle Kingdom (2040-1640 B.C.) and the New Kingdom (1552-1070 B.C.). Between these times the country was torn by civil war and after the New Kingdom it was invaded by Assyrians, Persians and Greeks.

Q Did they conquer other kingdoms?

A During the New Kingdom the pharoahs built up a powerful army of infantry and charioteers. They built an empire which stretched from Syria in the north to Sudan in the south.

Q Was the River Nile important?

A Not only did the River Nile give the Egyptians fish and duck to eat, its annual flooding left a rich layer of silt on its banks which made the soil fertile again. Papyrus reeds grew in the river. These could be made into baskets, mats, brushes and paper. The river also made trade possible as it could be used to transport goods, even heavy objects such as stone. Around ninety percent of Egyptians lived within 6 mi. of the Nile or its marshy delta.

Q Did Egypt trade with other countries?

A Egypt traded gold in return for cedar wood from Lebanon, and oil, wine and silver from lands further afield. Ebony, ivory and incense came from countries south of Egypt.

What was life like in Egypt?

Egyptian mothers gave their children beer to take to school for their lunch.

Historians have a good idea what life was like in Egypt thanks to documents written on papyrus, inscriptions on stone and wall paintings and objects found in tombs.

Q What did people wear?

A Due to the hot climate, people needed only light clothes, usually made of linen. Often clothes were not worn indoors. Slaves, laborers and children usually went naked. However, people cared very much about their appearance and keeping clean. Both men and women wore eye makeup, jewelery and perfume.

Q How did they amuse themselves?

A Wall paintings show women dancing and having picnics, and men wrestling and hunting duck, antelopes and hares. Board games were popular with adults as well as children, and many families kept pets.

Q What were their houses like?

A Homes, and even royal palaces, were made from sun-dried mud bricks. Stone was only used for tombs and temples. The hot weather and bright light meant that windows were small and placed high in the wall. Doors and windows often had screens made of matting to keep out flies and dust. In the hottest weather people slept on the flat roof.

Q Did people eat well?

A The Nile provided fish, eels, ducks and geese. Fruit, vegetables and pork were also important parts of the daily diet. The Egyptians introduced the watermelon from southern Africa and the fig from Turkey. They also knew how to make wine, beer and cheese. Wheat was used to make pastry and biscuits, often flavored with honey and herbs, and forty different kinds of bread.

Egyptian gods. From left to right: Hathor, Toth, Anubis, Osiris and Isis.

Q Was religion important?

A The fact that the Egyptians built so many huge temples shows that religion was very important to them. They worshipped many different gods and believed that there was life after death. This belief led them to preserve the bodies of the dead as mummies, and to bury them with food, tools and weapons for the afterlife. Priests were very powerful. Ordinary people believed they could tell the future from dreams and the stars, and even protect them from evil with charms and spells.

Q What work did people do?

A Most people were farmers. When there was no work in the fields they had time to help with the building of temples or pyramids. This was also a way of paying taxes. Skilled craftsmen were well paid, but they were paid in food, linen, firewood or salt, rather than money. Most women looked after their families, but they could also be weavers, dancers, nannies, priestesses, or makers of perfume and makeup.

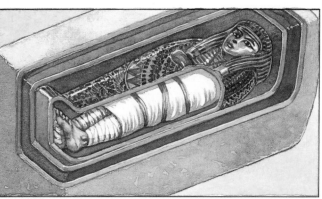

Q How were bodies made into mummies?

A The body was cut open and the heart, lungs and other organs were taken out and kept separately in a set of jars. The brain was pulled out through the nose with a hook, bit by bit, and thrown away. The body was then filled with natron, a natural salt which dried it out and stopped it from rotting. It was then stuffed with cloths and rolled in bandages before being buried inside two or three coffins. The whole business took about seventy days.

Q When did people work?

A People worked for eight days at a time and then had two days rest. There were also 65 holy days set aside for ceremonies and festivals. People also took time off for funerals and birthdays. Most work was done in two shifts during the cooler times of the day - morning and evening. People took a nap during the heat of midday.

The pyramids at Giza once had smooth sides but the outer stones have been removed, leaving the step shape we see today.

What can be seen of Ancient Egypt?

Egypt's dry desert air has preserved many of its ancient treasures. Modern Egypt's tourist industry is based on taking visitors to famous sites and museums.

Q Why were the pyramids built?

A Pyramids were built to guard the bodies of dead pharaohs and their treasures. The first pyramids were built before the Old Kingdom and had sides rising in steps. The pyramids at Giza were built during the Old Kingdom, and are the only one of the Seven Wonders of the Ancient World which can be seen today.

Q Which was the biggest pyramid?

A The pyramid built for Khufu is 755.9 ft. along each side and was originally 469 ft. high. Its four sides face exactly north, south, east and west. Around 2,300,000 blocks of stone were needed to build it, each one averaging over two tons and the largest weighing 17 tons. It took 100,000 men over twenty years to build it.

Q Who was Tutankhamun?

A Tutankhamun became pharaoh when he was nine years old and died at the age of nineteen in 1352 B.C. His tomb was discovered in 1922. Unlike almost all the other royal tombs it had not been robbed and was filled with wonderful treasures.

Here are the Karnak Ruins, which were once the royal treasury, form the largest group of ancient buildings in the world.

Q How did the Egyptians write?

A The Egyptians wrote in hieroglyphs, which were pictures of objects but could also be used to represent sounds. There were over 700 hieroglyphs.

Q What is the Rosetta Stone?

A The Rosetta Stone is a carved stone tablet with an inscription in Greek and hieroglyphic writing. It helped experts to understand hieroglyphics.

Q Is the Nile still important?

A The Nile is still vital to Egypt. Over ninety percent of the people still live along its banks or in its delta. The annual flood is now controlled by the High Dam at Aswan. This allows the water to be used more efficiently and some has been diverted for farming. The dam also generates electricity for industry.

Q What are the main sites that visitors can see?

A Near the ruins of Thebes are the temples of Luxor and Karnak, linked by an avenue of sphinxes 1.8 mi. long. On the south side of the Nile lies the "Valley of the Kings," where Tutankhamun's tomb was found. At Abu Simbel, near the border with Sudan, two massive temples in honor of Ramesses II were cut out of a sandstone cliff.

Greek merchants traded
all over the Aegean,
Mediterranean and
Black Seas.

Who were the Greeks?

They set up many
important colonies
where they traded.

The Greeks lived in separate city states, scattered from southern Russia to Spain. Greek civilization flourished between 800 B.C. and 500 B.C. By 30 B.C. the Romans had taken over the Greek Empire

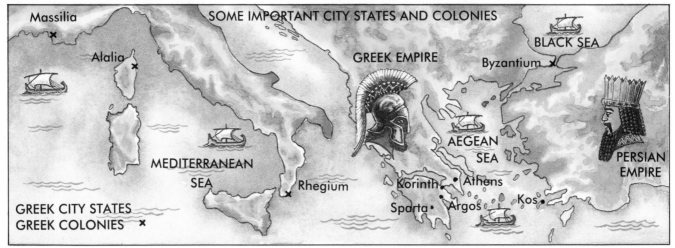

SOME IMPORTANT CITY STATES AND COLONIES

Massilia

Alalia

BLACK SEA

GREEK EMPIRE

Byzantium

MEDITERRANEAN
SEA

AEGEAN
SEA

PERSIAN
EMPIRE

Rhegium

Korinth   Athens

GREEK CITY STATES

Sparta   Argos   Kos

GREEK COLONIES

Q What was a city state?

A Each city state consisted of a city and the land surrounding it. They had their own government, army and money system. Most of them were situated near the sea and traded with each other.

Q Which were the most important city states?

A The leading city state was Athens. Athens had rich silver mines, a big navy and factories making things such as weapons, furniture, pottery and leather goods. The main rival to Athens was Sparta. Sparta was a warlike city state where every citizen served in the army.

Q How big was Athens?

A Athens had a territory of about 617 sq. mi. and a population of around 200,000. Only about 40,000 of these were free men, who fought in the army and took part in government. The rest were women, children, slaves and foreigners, all of whom had fewer rights than the Athenian men.

Q How did the Greeks fight?

A The main strength of the Greek armies was the infantry. Soldiers wore a helmet, leg guards called greaves, and a bronze breastplate. They were armed with a sword and a 21 foot spear called a sarissa. They also carried a large round shield. These soldiers were organized into disciplined groups called phalanxes. The Greeks also had a cavalry and a navy.

Q Who were the Greek's main enemies?

A The powerful Persian Empire was the main threat to the Greeks. Between 490 B.C. and 479 B.C. the Greeks united to defeat two large Persian invasions. Sometimes the different city states fought each other. Athens and Sparta had a long war with each other, from 431 B.C. to 404 B.C., which Sparta eventually won.

Q Who was Alexander the Great?

A Alexander was the King of Macedonia. He built a huge empire, stretching from Greece to the borders of India. He founded many cities, and spread the Greek culture through the Middle East. Alexander died in 323 B.C. at the age of 33.

Q What were Greek warships like?

A The most powerful warship was the trireme, which had three rows of oars, rowed by 170 men. It used sails when possible, but used its oars during calm weather or when it was going to ram another ship with its 9.8 ft. ram. It could travel at up to 9 mph.

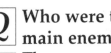

How did the Greeks live?

The Greeks used inflated pig's bladders to play football.

Lots of writers used to live in Athens, so much is known about the way people lived at this time.

Q Did people eat well?

A Greek food was plain but healthy - fish, barley bread, goat's cheese, olives, figs, fruit, vegetables and salads flavored with parsley or basil. Meat was only eaten at festivals. Poor people ate lupins, a kind of flower, and grasshoppers.

Q What did Greeks learn at school?

A Apart from teaching how to read and write, schools also taught poetry, music and physical education. The Greeks thought that the ideal man should be able to fight, make speeches and entertain his friends. Girls did not go to school but learned how to spin and weave from their mothers.

Q How did people travel?

A Donkeys were used to carry people and goods short distances. As Greece is so mountainous it was usually easier to travel longer distances by boat around the coast rather than go overland.

Q How did women live?

A Women in Athens played little part in public life, except at religious festivals. They got married at age 13 or 14 and spent most of their time at home. They were allowed to own clothes, jewels and slaves; but not land or houses. Women in Sparta were treated equally to men and could own land, but they did not fight in the army.

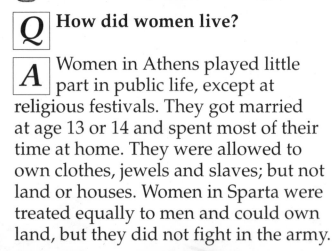

Q What sort of religion did the Greeks have?

A The Greeks worshipped many gods and their greatest buildings were temples put up in honor of the gods. Only priests were allowed inside the temples. Sacrifices and other ceremonies were held outside.

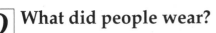

Q What did people wear?

A The main item of clothing that men and women wore was the tunic. They also wore woolen cloaks, straw hats and leather sandals. Rich Greeks could afford silk clothes and expensive dyes to color their clothes, but most people wore lightweight linen and woolen clothes. Brooches and pins were used to hold clothes in place as buttons were not used.

Q What gods did they worship?

A The Greeks believed that the gods lived on Mount Olympus, the highest mountain in Greece. The most powerful god was Zeus, king of the gods. There were gods or goddesses for every aspect of life, such as war, love, music and hunting.

Zeus

Athena

Hera

Hermes

Only men were allowed to act in Greek plays. All actors wore masks.

Greek culture has had a lasting effect on later European history, in both the arts and sciences.

Q Did the Greeks make any scientific discoveries?

A The Greeks developed the scientific ideas that they discovered in Babylon and Egypt. For example, they knew that the Earth traveled around the Sun. They also invented steam engines. The ideas of Pythagoras and Euclid are still taught today.

Q What was the importance of Greek art and architecture?

A The Greek style of building was copied by the Romans and has been used by architects ever since, especially for public buildings, such as museums and town halls. Greek buildings were often decorated with bronze or marble statues. Many of these statues can be seen in museums all around the world.

Q Did the Greeks have myths and legends?

A The Greeks had many stories about heroes, such as Herakles (Hercules). There are also many stories about monsters, like the bull-headed Minotaur, the one-eyed Cyclops and the Gorgon, called Medusa, who could turn people to stone. These stories have been retold ever since Greek times.

The Greeks dated their history from 776 B.C., when the first Olympics were held.

Q How did the Greeks cure their sick?

A The Greeks were one of the first peoples to cure the sick using herbs, baths, exercise and diet rather than rely on so-called magic spells. Hippocrates of Kos (460-357 B.C.) is the most famous of all the Greek doctors. His ideas were still being studied 2,000 years after his death.

Q Did the Greeks go to the theater?

A The theater was very popular in Ancient Greece. The theater at Epidaurus could seat 14,000 people. "Drama," "theatre," "comedy," "chorus," "scenery," "tragedy" and "orchestra" are all originally Greek words. Many Greek plays by Athenian writers such as Sophokles are still put on today.

Q Did the Greeks play sports?

A The Greeks took sports very seriously. Running, wrestling and throwing the javelin were good training for war. Festivals, called games, were held every four years at four separate sites around Greece. The games at Olympia were the most important. The competitions included poetry and music as well as athletics. Only men were allowed into the games The modern Olympics were based on these games and were first held in Athens in 1896.

54

The cavalry in the Roman army was usually made up of non-Romans. They were called auxiliaries.

How big was the Roman Empire?

The Roman Empire covered all of the Mediterranean, much of Europe and even north Africa. It began around 753 B.C. and lasted over one thousand years.

 Q Who founded Rome?

A According to Roman legend the twins Romulus and Remus founded Rome. As babies they were left to die, but were saved and cared for by wolves. The legend says they founded Rome in 753 B.C., with Romulus naming the city after himself and becoming the first king. However, historians think that the first kings were probably Etruscans who founded the city on the seven hills by the Tiber River in the seventh century B.C.

Q Who were the Etruscans?

A Very little is known about the Etruscans as their language is still not properly understood. Originally, they came from Turkey, and were at their height of power around 550 B.C. They were an advanced civilization which, amongst other things, wore robes like Roman togas and built the first drains in Rome.

Q How did Rome grow?

A At first Rome was only a weak city state. The Romans built a wall around the seven hills to defend themselves and built up a strong army. By 264 B.C. they had conquered all of Italy.

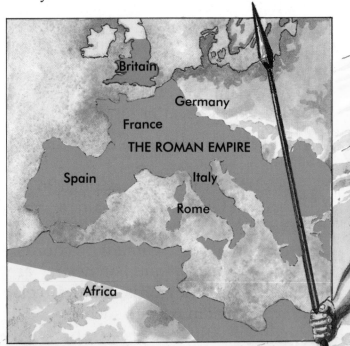

Britain

Germany

France

THE ROMAN EMPIRE

Spain

Italy

Rome

Africa

Q What were the Punic Wars?

A Rome's expansion brought it into conflict with the empire of Carthage (see page 12). Between 264 B.C. and 146 B.C. Rome fought three long wars with Carthage ending in total victory for Rome. In the course of these wars Rome conquered Sicily, Sardinia, Corsica, Spain and southern France.

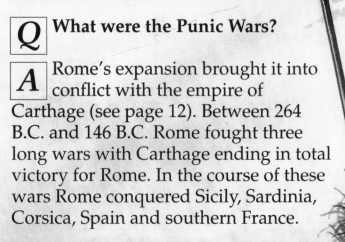

All Roman roads had milestones which measured the distance from the city of Rome.

Q Why was the Roman army important?

A The army conquered Rome's empire and defended it against its enemies. The main strength of the army was the infantry who often won against much larger numbers because they were so well armed, trained and disciplined. They were also good at building fortifications and besieging cities.

Q Why were Roman roads important?

A The Romans built excellent roads which allowed their soldiers to move quickly between forts and boundaries. Merchants also used the roads, so trade flourished. There were over 52,800 mi. of roads which were so well built that they lasted for centuries.

Julius Caesar

Q Who was Julius Caesar?

A Julius Caesar was a famous general who conquered most of France. He was also a good public speaker and was popular with Romans. He made himself ruler of Rome, but was murdered by former friends who thought that Rome should be a republic and not ruled by one man.

Julius Caesar changed the calendar from 355 days a year to the 365-day system we use now.

What was life like in Rome?

A million people lived in Rome in A.D. 200. However, not everyone was well off. By A.D. 270, around 300,000 people were unemployed and lived on free handouts of barley bread, pork fat and olive oil from the government.

Q What did people eat?

A Rich Romans ate ham from Gaul or oysters from Britannia and spiced their food with pepper from India or ginger from China. Rice, sugar and carrots were known of but rarely eaten. Sheep and goat's milk was preferred to cow's milk. Poor people ate bean soup.

Q What were their homes like?

A Poor people lived in badly-built apartment blocks without bathrooms or kitchens. They used public baths and got hot food from cook-shops. The houses of rich Romans faced inwards on to an open space, called an atrium, with arcades to provide shade from the hot sun. Rich people often had big villas and estates in the country.

Q How did people keep clean and healthy?

A All Roman cities had public baths, like modern leisure centers, where people could bathe and swim. Romans also visited the baths to work out at the gymnasium, watch acrobats, gamble or chat with friends and buy snacks.

The Romans introduced football to Britain in A.D. 200.

Q Who did all the work?

A Nearly one third of the population were slaves, who did all the work. If they were educated they might have a comfortable life as a tutor, book keeper, doctor, or musician with a wealthy family. However, farmers, laborers and miners had a hard life and usually a short one.

Q What entertainments were there?

A As slaves did most of the work, many Roman citizens had time for leisure. Like the Greeks, they enjoyed the theater. The word "pantomime" comes from the Roman word for a mimed show. Even more popular were games which included chariot racing and combats in which gladiators fought each other or wild beasts.

Q What did the Romans believe in?

A The Romans adopted many Greek gods. They called Zeus "Jupiter," Poseidon "Neptune," Hermes "Mercury," and Aphrodite "Venus." Emperors were worshipped as gods after their death. When they came to live in a colony such as Britain, they often added in local gods as well. Romans also believed in household spirits, and in fortune telling through astrology, dice, palm reading, sacrifices and interpreting natural events, like lightning or flocks of birds.

Q How were people punished?

A The Romans had a very complicated system of law. Punishments for law breaking or minor offences, included fines or whipping . Major crimes might lead to loss of citizenship, banishment to a distant place or being sent to work in a mine or as a galley slave. Execution might be by beheading, drowning, crucifixion or being made to fight in the games. Prisons were only used to detain people until they were punished in some other way.

The word "pen" comes from the Latin for feather.

What was the impact of Roman rule?

Roman rule had its greatest impact in northwest Europe, where Romans built the first cities and roads. Roman rule had less impact in Greece, Egypt and the Middle East where there were already long established civilizations.

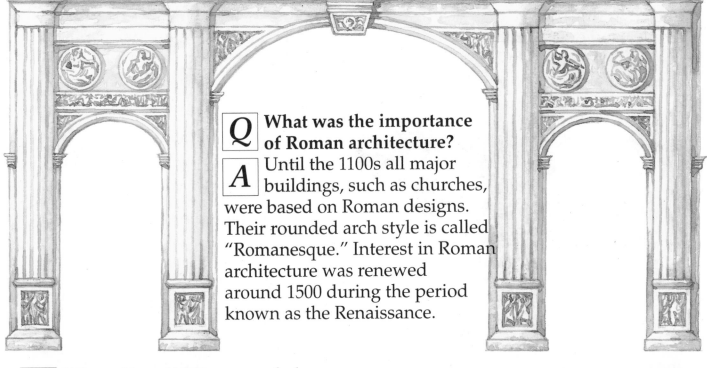

Q What was the importance of Roman architecture?

A Until the 1100s all major buildings, such as churches, were based on Roman designs. Their rounded arch style is called "Romanesque." Interest in Roman architecture was renewed around 1500 during the period known as the Renaissance.

Q What effect did Roman rule have on Europe?

A Many of the main roads in Europe still follow the lines of old Roman roads. Also, many place names are linked to their Roman past. For example place names in England ending in -caster or -chester come from "castra," the Latin word for a military camp or fort.

Only the Roman emperor and his family were allowed to wear purple cloth.

Q How did Roman rule affect Christianity?

A Roman emperors often persecuted Christians because they refused to worship them as gods. However the emperor, Constantine, had a Christian mother, and Christianity then became the official religion of the empire.

Q Why was Latin important?

A After Roman rule had ended Latin was used as the written language of learning, government and religion throughout most of Europe for a thousand years. Over the same period Latin as a spoken language developed into Italian, French, Spanish, Portugese and Romanian. English, which developed from German, has thousands of words from Latin.

Q How has Roman history inspired art and literature?

A Roman history has inspired artists and historians for centuries. Shakespeare wrote the plays *Julius Ceasar* and *Antony and Cleopatra* a thousand years after the Romans left Britain. More recently the nineteenth century novels *Quo Vadis* and *The Last Days of Pompeii* have been made into films.

Q Where can Roman remains be seen today?

A Impressive ruins can be seen in most of the countries around the Mediterranean Sea. The Colosseum and Pantheon are two of the most impressive ruins in Rome. Pompeii, a Roman town, was preserved under a layer of volcanic ash when Mount Vesuvius erupted in A.D. 79. There are also many important remains in Britain such as Hadrian's Wall and Fishbourne Villa.

Who were the first explorers?

To frighten off other travelers, the Phoenicians spread tales of sea serpents.

Phoenicians ruled the Mediterranean for one thousand years from 1400 B.C.

The earliest explorers lived in pre-historic times, more than half a million years ago. They were Stone Age people in the land now called Africa, searching for new sources of food and shelter.

Q Why did people begin to explore?

A Exploration was often a question of survival. People hoped to find fresh supplies of food and living materials and often a safer place away from enemies.

Q What were the earliest boats made from?

A Boats might have been made from hollowed-out logs, reeds, or skins stretched over a wooden frame.

Q How did people first explore?

A The first explorers probably traveled on foot or on horseback. But it was easier to travel greater distances across the sea or along rivers by boat.

Q Who were the greatest early explorers to cross oceans?

A The Phoenicians, who lived in what is now Israel, built a large fleet of ships around 800 B.C. They traveled as far as Africa and the British Isles to trade.

Q What cargoes did ships carry?

A Egyptian ships carried wood, ivory, silver, gold, cloth and spices. They also carried animals.

Q Who first sailed around Africa?

A The dangerous journey around what is now called the Cape of Good Hope was made by the Phoenicians in about 600 B.C.

In about 1500 B.C., Queen Hatshepsut of Egypt sent five ships to Punt (now called Somalia) for spices, monkeys, dogs and minerals.

Q Who was the most famous of the early explorers?

A Alexander the Great was a famous Greek general and explorer. He explored in order to conquer. By 326 B.C. his conquests stretched from Egypt in the West to northern India in the East.

Viking sailors sometimes relied on the instinct of birds. From time to time they would release a raven and follow it, hoping it would lead them to

Before modern instruments such as radar and radio were invented, explorers had to use other methods to discover their position at sea and in strange lands.

About 3,000 years ago, Polynesians were exploring the Pacific Islands in canoes. To navigate they studied the positions of the stars, wind direction and the pattern of ocean waves.

Q How did the earliest explorers navigate?

A Navigators studied the position of the Moon, Sun and stars. Some also knew how to sail along a given latitude (distance north or south of a line called the Equator which runs around the middle of the Earth).

Q How did explorers find remote islands?

A Early sailors could guess where land lay from the behavior of sea creatures and from the shape and size of waves. Their boats may have been carried across the ocean by currents.

Q How did sailors know they were near land if they didn't have a chart?

A Sailors knew they were near land when they saw birds or floating vegetation. Sometimes the color of the sea or the shape of clouds changed near land.

The telescope was invented in the early seventeenth century.

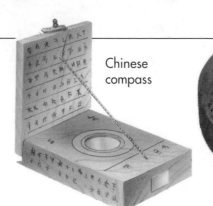

Chinese compass

 Q | **Who invented the compass?**

A | The Chinese invented the first compass about 4,000 years ago. However, European explorers did not use them until about 1,000 years ago.

A compass consists of a magnetized needle on a pivot. Because of the Earth's magnetism, the needle always points to magnetic north.

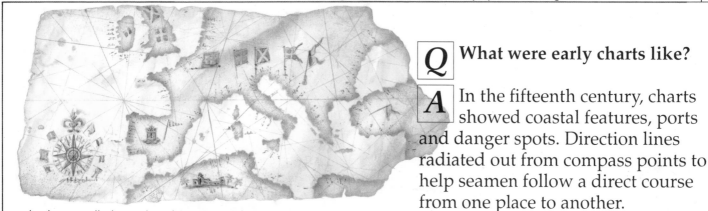

Early charts, called portulan charts, were drawn on stretched animal skin (parchment).

Q | **What were early charts like?**

A | In the fifteenth century, charts showed coastal features, ports and danger spots. Direction lines radiated out from compass points to help seamen follow a direct course from one place to another.

Q | **What was a quadrant used for?**

A | The quadrant was the earliest instrument used to measure the height of the Sun or stars. It was invented by the Arabs. In the fifteenth century, seamen used it to work out their latitude.

The sights of a quadrant were lined up with the Sun or a star. The plumb line showed the number of degrees above the horizon to work out a ship's position at sea.

Q | **What was an astrolabe?**

A | Like the quadrant, the astrolabe was used to work out latitude. Both instruments were fairly inaccurate at sea, when readings were taken on a rolling deck.

Astrolabes were made of brass. There were two holes at either end of the arm, which were lined up so the Sun or a star shone through. The arm then showed the height above the horizon.

Some Vikings dared to sail into the unknown Atlantic - to the Faroes, Iceland, Greenland and even America.

How far did the Vikings travel?

Longships were shallow in depth, so Vikings could sail a long way up rivers and estuaries.

The Viking Age began around A.D. 800 and lasted about three hundred years. Vikings explored many distant lands including parts of Russia and North America.

Q Why did the Vikings search for new lands?

A Scandinavia, where the Vikings came from, has long, cold winters and much of the land is difficult to farm. Large families could not grow enough food, so new places to live had to be found.

Q Which was the first Viking colony?

A The Vikings first discovered Iceland in A.D. 860 when a group of explorers were blown off course. Irish monks had already reached the island about sixty-five years earlier.

Q What were Viking ships like?

A Vikings warships were known as longships. These were fast, sleek ships, well suited to raiding and long-distance travel.

Cross-section of a longship

Q What goods did the Vikings traders want?

A They wanted gold, silver, spices, silk, jewelery and iron.

Q Where did the Vikings go?

A The Vikings raided France, Britain and Ireland. They sailed around Spain and into the Mediterranean. Vikings journeyed down the great rivers of Russia to reach the Caspian Sea and the Black Sea. They also crossed the Atlantic to North America.

Q Where did the crew sleep?

A There were no cabins on Viking ships. Viking sailors just covered themselves with animal hides or blankets, though some ships had awnings (roof-coverings). Voyages were not normally made in the coldest winter months .

Q Where did Vikings put their cargo?

A Viking ships did not have decks. Cargo was stored on the floor in the middle of the ship between the oarsmen who sat in the bow and stern.

Knarrs were probably no more than 60 ft. long.

On voyages Vikings ate smoked fish, dried meat and vegetables.

Q What were Viking cargo ships like?

A Vikings carried cargo in ships called knarrs, which were wider than longships and mostly used for coastal trading.

Arab merchants who traded with India and the Far East were incredibly rich.

Who were the first Arab explorers?

Arabs played an important part in the history of exploration. In the sixth and seventh centuries they conquered a huge empire, spreading education and Islam.

Q What sort of ships did Arabs have?

A Arab ships were known as dhows. They had triangular sails, and needed only a small crew.

Q Where did Arab explorers learn about navigation?

A Arabs learned about navigation in the Indian Ocean while on trading missions. They worked out how to find their way by the stars. They also learned about tides, ocean currents and the monsoon cycle (heavy rainstorms).

Q Did Arab explorers make maps?

A Yes. There is a famous map of about 1150 made on a silver tablet by an explorer called Idrisi. He was a Spanish-born Arab who visited France and England as well as the East.

Early maps included only the top of Africa. The ship-like figure on the left is meant to show three lakes feeding into the River Nile.

Q Who was the greatest Arab explorer?

A The most famous Arab explorer was Ibn Batuta from Tangier in North Africa. He visited many countries from 1325 to 1355.

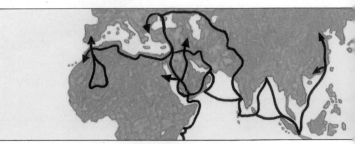

Stories about Arab merchants inspired many adventure stories, including *Sinbad the Sailor* and *The Thousand and One Nights*.

CHINA

AFRICA

INDIAN OCEAN

Dhows are still used in the Indian Ocean today.

Q **Where did Arab merchants travel to?**

A From the 7th to 9th centuries, they reached India, China, Russia, southern Africa and Zanzibar (Tanzania).

Q **How did European knowledge compare with that of the Arabs?**

A Europeans knew less about science, mathematics and geography than the Arabs. Their view of the world was restricted by Christian beliefs. On European maps the Earth was shown as a circle with Jerusalem at its center.

China Asia India
Tower of Babel
Europe Jerusalem
Africa

Q **Was there any region where Arab explorers were afraid to go?**

A Arabs called the Atlantic "The Sea of Darkness." Idrisi may have sailed into it, but if he did he was the only Arab who dared to do so.

Ibn Batuta traveled about 74,500 mi. during his thirty years of voyages.

Q **How did the West come to share Arab learning?**

A Christian knights came into contact with the Arabs during the Crusades (1096-1291) when the Christians tried to win back Jerusalem. Arabs had also conquered much of Spain.

Marco Polo

Kublai Khan

Who first made contact with China?

China, in the Far East, was a difficult place to reach. In 1271 Marco Polo, the son of a merchant from Venice, Italy, traveled overland to Peking (Beijing) with his father and uncle and spent many years with the Chinese emperor Kublai Khan.

Q What did merchants want from the Chinese?

A Western merchants wanted silk, spices and porcelain which they traded in return for gold and silver.

Q Why did Marco Polo travel to China?

A Marco's father, Niccolo, and his uncle, Maffeo, had already spent fifteen years in China. They returned to Italy and then, in 1271, decided to go back, taking Marco with them. They carried gifts from Pope Gregory X, who hoped the great Mongol leader Kublai Khan would recognize Christianity as superior to the many other religions in China.

Q How long did Marco stay in the Khan's court?

A The Khan kept Marco at his court for seventeen years, sending him on diplomatic missions all over China. Because of his quick grasp of languages and his skill at making notes on everything he saw, Marco was able to report back to Kublai Khan and, later, to people in Venice.

Q Were the Polo family the first Europeans to reach China?

A No. The route known as the Silk Road, which ran from China to the West, had been used by traders since about 500 B.C., but the Polos were the first Europeans to travel its entire length and make contact with Chinese leaders.

Venice

The Silk Road

Q How did the Polos travel to Shangdu, where Kublai Khan had his palace?

A They used camels to carry provisions through Armenia into Persia (Iran), through Afghanistan, the Gobi Desert and China. They traveled 6,959 mi., and took three-and-a-half years to reach Shangdu. On the way they spent a year in Kanchow learning the customs of the Mongol peoples.

Junks were flat-bottomed ships with sails made of matting stiffened with wooden strips. They could make long voyages.

Q How did Marco return?

A Marco was given the job of escorting a princess to Persia (Iran), where she was to marry a prince. After stopping at Sumatra, Java, Malaya, Ceylon (Sri Lanka) and India, he delivered the princess to Persia and sailed home to Venice.

The Silk Road was so dangerous that goods were passed along it from one merchant to another. No one before had travelled its entire length.

Shang-tu

PERSIA

The Chinese had already explored to the west. In the second century B.C. they reached Persia (Iran).

CHINA

Hormuz

Canton

INDIA

On his death bed, Marco Polo was asked to admit that he had been lying about his adventures. He replied "I have not told half of what I saw."

—— The Silk Road
- - - Marco Polo's Route

AFRICA

Q How did people learn of Marco's adventures?

A After Marco's return in 1295, war broke out between the Venetians and the Genoese, and he was taken prisoner. In prison he dictated his story to another prisoner. Many people did not believe his book, which described the discovery of oil, coal, magnificent palaces, parades of elephants, gifts to Kublai Khan of 100,000 white horses and huge jewels that were beyond the imagination of the Venetians.

Q What new sights did Marco see?

A On his travels Marco saw many strange and wonderful things unknown to Europeans. He marveled at the huge cities and strange-shaped ships on the great rivers. He saw, for the first time, people using paper money, burning coal not wood, and printing words on paper using wooden blocks. Marco also found sources of jewels and spices.

When was the Great Age of Exploration?

The fifteenth and early sixteenth centuries are often called the Great Age of Exploration because so many discoveries were made at this time. Sea routes were found to the East, and unknown lands were explored - for example, America, the West Indies and the Pacific.

Q Why were there so many explorers at this time?

A This was an exciting time of new learning. Western Europeans wanted to find out more about the world, and had developed ships that would allow them to do so. Merchants wanted to obtain such valuable things as spices, silk, gems and fine china. Spices from the East were needed for cooking and medicines.

Q Which country began the Great Age of Exploration?

A The Portugese, in the early fifteenth century. Ships sailing out of Lisbon port picked up strong winds which drove them directly south until they picked up a wind to drive them east.

Q Who first sailed round the southern tip of Africa?

A The Portuguese captain, Bartolomeo Dias did, in 1487. He had two caravels and a larger ship to carry stores. He sailed round the Cape of Good Hope but his crew refused to go any further.

Q Who paid for the expeditions?

A Usually they were sponsored by the royal family of a country. Prince Henry of Portugal became known as Henry the Navigator not because he ever went to sea, but because he sponsored Portuguese expeditions. Spanish and English kings and queens also paid for explorers' voyages. They wanted to find riches overseas and to gain power over any new lands that were discovered.

Q Which European first reached India by sea?

A The Portuguese sailor, Vasco da Gama did. He followed Dias' route around Africa. Then he took on board an Arab pilot who helped him navigate to India. Da Gama lost two ships and half his men, but took back to Portugal a cargo of spices and precious gems.

Many of Da Gama's men died of scurvy from not having enough fresh food.

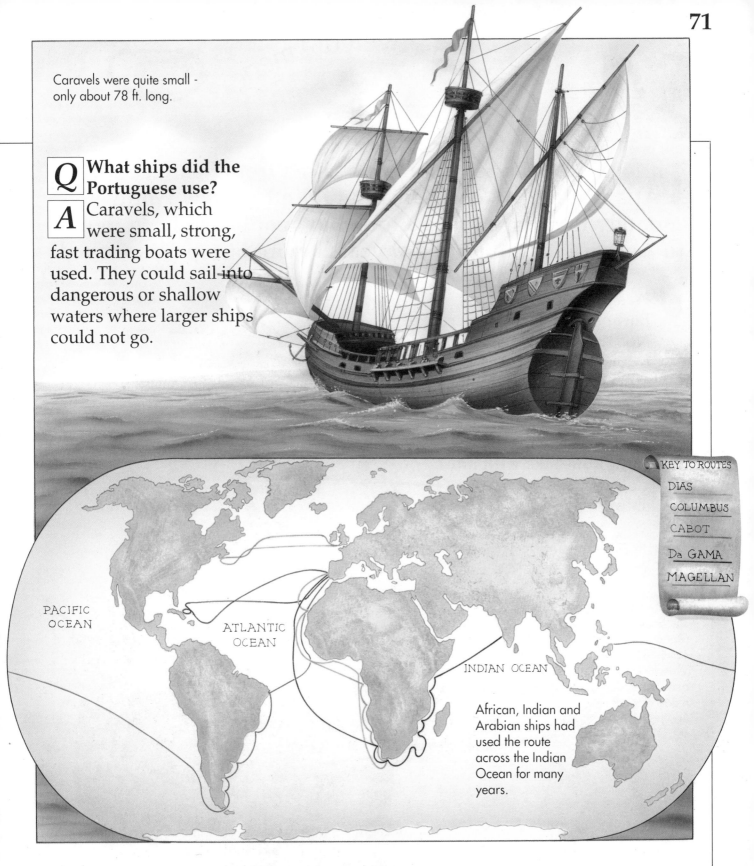

Caravels were quite small - only about 78 ft. long.

Q **What ships did the Portuguese use?**

A Caravels, which were small, strong, fast trading boats were used. They could sail into dangerous or shallow waters where larger ships could not go.

KEY TO ROUTES

DIAS

COLUMBUS

CABOT

Da GAMA

MAGELLAN

PACIFIC OCEAN

ATLANTIC OCEAN

INDIAN OCEAN

African, Indian and Arabian ships had used the route across the Indian Ocean for many years.

Q **Which were the most exciting years of the Great Age of Exploration?**

A A These major discoveries were made within the astonishingly short space of thirty-four years:

1487 Dias sailed around the tip of Africa.
1492 Columbus reached the West Indies.
1497 The English explorer John Cabot reached Newfoundland, off North America.
1498 Da Gama reached India by sea.
1519-21 Magellan sailed into the Pacific.

Who discovered America?

In 1492 Christopher Columbus sailed from Spain across the Atlantic to the West Indies and found a "New World" that nobody in Europe knew about. But people had been living in America for thousands of years before Europeans arrived.

Q Was Columbus the first European to sail to America?

A No. The Vikings had probably reached America in A.D. 985, but their voyages had been long forgotten when Columbus sailed.

Q How many ships did Columbus take with him?

A Columbus took three ships on his first voyage - the *Santa Maria* (his flagship), the *Nina* and the *Pinta*.

The Santa Maria hit a coral reef in the West Indies, so only two ships made it back to Spain.

Columbus was a brave man. Da Gama knew that India existed, though he was not sure how to reach it. Columbus was sailing into the unknown.

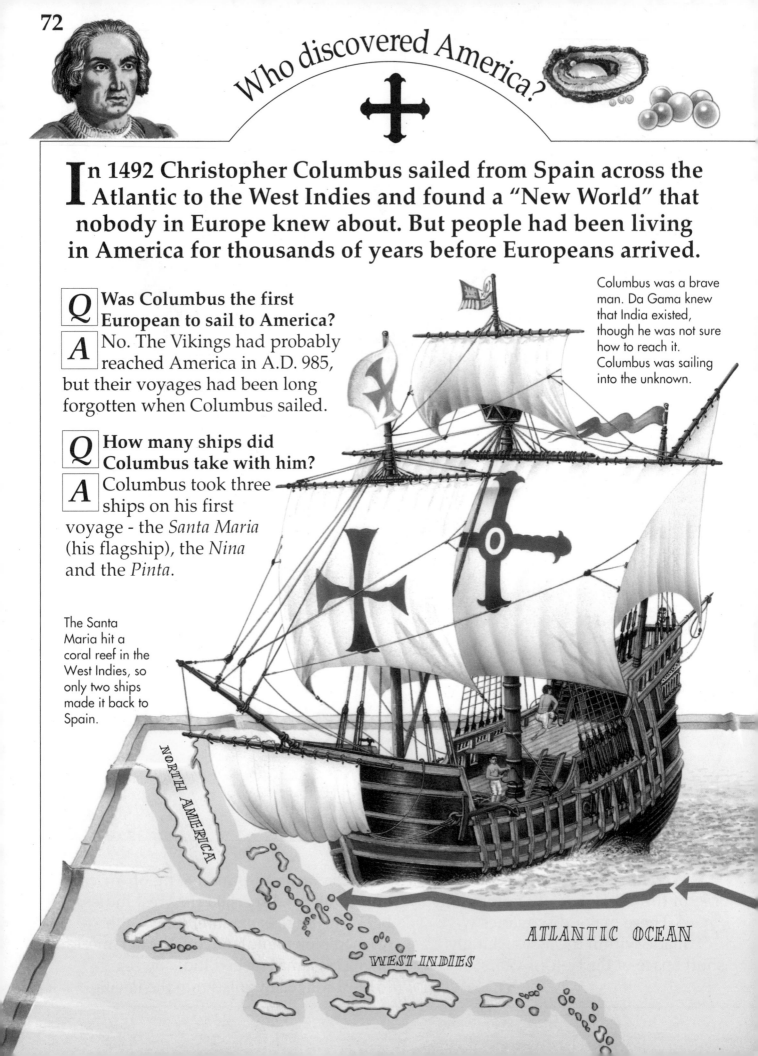

NORTH AMERICA

ATLANTIC OCEAN

WEST INDIES

Columbus found pearls in the West Indies. This made him believe he had reached China as Marco Polo's book had mentioned the Chinese diving for pearls.

Q Where did Columbus believe he was going?

A He thought he was going to China. When he got to the West Indies he insisted they were islands off China.

Q What did Columbus expect to find?

A He expected to find gold, pearls and spices because they were all mentioned in Marco Polo's book on China.

Q Why were Columbus's crews frightened on the voyage?

A They thought they were going too far from home and that in the Atlantic no wind ever blew in the direction of Spain, so they might never return!

Q Where does the name "America" come from?

A It comes from Amerigo Vespucci, an Italian adventurer, who claimed that he reached the mainland of America in 1497, but it is doubtful that he did so.

Q Did Columbus actually set foot in America?

A No. He first landed in the West Indies. Later, he made three more voyages to the West Indies. On his third voyage he reached Panama, in Central America, but he never landed on the mainland of North America.

Columbus believed the world was round, so you could reach the East by sailing west. His mistake was to think the world was smaller than it is. He thought the distance from Europe to Asia was 3,550 mi. In fact it is 11,766 mi.

Each day Columbus lied to his men about the distance they had traveled because they were afraid of sailing too far from Spain.

SPAIN

Palos

AFRICA

Who first sailed around the world?

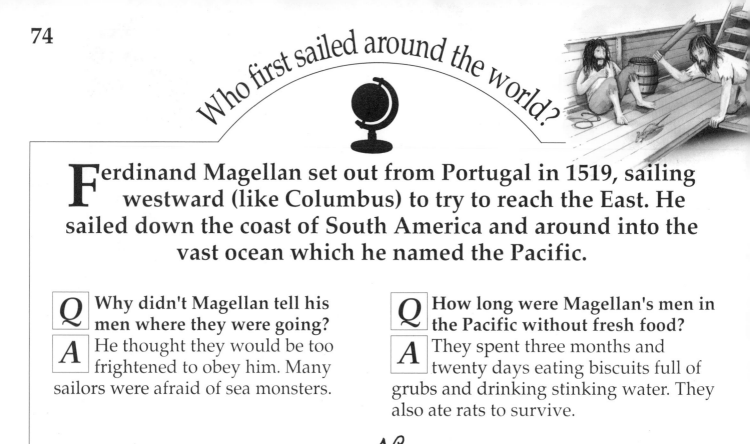

Ferdinand Magellan set out from Portugal in 1519, sailing westward (like Columbus) to try to reach the East. He sailed down the coast of South America and around into the vast ocean which he named the Pacific.

Q Why didn't Magellan tell his men where they were going?

A He thought they would be too frightened to obey him. Many sailors were afraid of sea monsters.

Q How long were Magellan's men in the Pacific without fresh food?

A They spent three months and twenty days eating biscuits full of grubs and drinking stinking water. They also ate rats to survive.

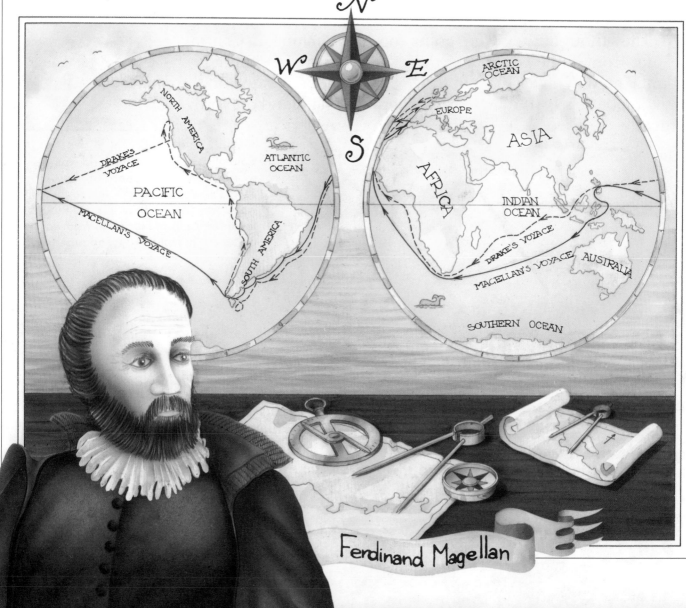

Ferdinand Magellan

Many sailors died of hunger and disease because they did not have fresh food supplies.

Q How was the passage to the Pacific discovered?

A Two of Magellan's ships were blown in a storm toward the South American coast. Just in time the crews spotted a small opening. It was the strait (passage) they were looking for. It is now called the Strait of Magellan.

Q Did Magellan actually sail around the world?

A No, he was killed in a battle with islanders in the Philippines.

Q How many men returned safely?

A Of the 260 or so crew aboard five ships who set out, only 18 men and one ship, the *Vittoria*, returned to Spain in 1522. They were the first people to sail right around the world.

Q What "strange" creatures did they see?

A In St. Julian Bay, South America, Magellan's men described seeing strange birds, seawolves with webbed paws at their sides, and camels without humps. These were probably puffins, seals and llamas.

Q Who led the second voyage around the world?

A Sir Francis Drake, who left Britain in 1577 to rob Spanish treasure ships did. Following Magellan's route around South America, he returned to England in 1580.

Sir Francis Drake

Who were the "conquistadors?"

Spaniards were appalled by the idol worship and human sacrifice they found in Mexico and Peru.

Once Columbus had successfully sailed across the Atlantic, Spaniards began to explore Central America. Adventurers came to the Americas to make their fortunes. These men became known as *conquistadors* (which is Spanish for conquerors).

EMPIRE OF THE AZTECS

CENTRAL AMERICA

SOUTH AMERICA

EMPIRE OF THE INCAS

Cortes

Q What did the conquistadors want?

A They wanted land, gold and other riches. They also wanted to convert the native Americans to Christianity.

Aztecs did not have horses or firearms. This helped Cortes to win.

Q Who already lived in South America?

A Many native peoples, including the Aztecs, who ruled in Mexico, and the Incas who ruled in Peru did.

Q Who conquered the Aztecs?

A The Spaniard, Hernando Cortes, landed in Mexico in 1519 with 600 soldiers and sixteen horses.

Aztecs thought one of their gods, Quetzalcoatl, had a white face and black beard - like Cortes. They believed he wore a feathered headdress, and Cortes wore a feather in his helmet.

Spaniards took cows, horses and pigs to South America.

Q **How did Cortes win with so few men?**

A The Aztec emperor, Montezuma, thought that Cortes might be a god and so did not fight. Later, other tribes who did not like the Aztecs helped Cortes.

Thousands of Aztecs died of European diseases that the Spanish brought with them, such as smallpox, measles and colds.

Q **What happened to the Incas?**

A Another Spaniard, Francisco Pizarro, defeated the Incas in 1531-33 with a small army. He captured their king, said he would release him in return for a roomful of gold, then murdered the king anyway

Red Pepper

Cacao Bean

Tomato

Potato

Turkey

When Drake returned to England in 1586, he brought news of tobacco, the Spanish name for a herb the Indians

Q **What happened to the Aztecs?**

A The Spaniards made the Aztecs slaves. They forced them to work hard in mines and on the land. Many died and within a few years the Aztec culture was destroyed.

Q **What new items came to Europe from the New World?**

A Tomatoes, chocolate (from the cacao bean) and red peppers came from America, as well as tobacco, potatoes and turkeys.

Who discovered Australia?

For a long time, geographers thought that there must be a southern continent to balance the weight of Europe and Asia, north of the Equator. They called this land Terra Australis Nondum Cognita (southern land not yet known).

Cook thought kangaroos looked like dogs, except that they jumped like hares.

Q Who first reached Australia?

A Aboriginal peoples have been living in Australia for thousands of years. The first European to sail there was a Dutch explorer, Willem Jansz, who reached the northern tip of Australia in 1606. Soon after, other Dutch ships explored the south seas, including, in 1642, Abel Tasman. He discovered Tasmania and went on to reach New Zealand.

Q Which explorers first saw kangaroos?

A Cook's crew saw kangaroos when the *Endeavour* ran aground off eastern Australia and took seven weeks to repair.

On long voyages, sailors usually got scurvy because they ate little fresh food and few vegetables. Cook made sure his men ate healthily.

Q Who first landed on the east coast of Australia?

A Captain James Cook, on the east coast in 1770. The British Admiralty had sent him on a voyage of exploration.

FLINDER'S ROUTE

When Flinders got back, his ship was so rotten he could push a stick right through the bottom timbers.

Q **Who first sailed right around Australia?**

A A British naval officer, Matthew Flinders, between 1801 and 1803, discovered how big Australia is, but his crew caught scurvy and his own health was damaged.

In 1860, Robert Burke and Charles Wills had tried to cross Australia from south to north. They got within sound of the sea, but had to turn back and died on the way.

BURKE AND WILLS ROUTE

STUART'S ROUTE

Q **Who first crossed Australia from south to north?**

A John Stuart, a Scotsman, crossed from Adelaide to Darwin in 1862. As a reward, he won a prize of £10,000 offered by the Australian government.

Stuart was so exhausted he had to be carried back in a sling tied between two horses.

Q **Why did early settlers in the east keep to the coastal areas?**

A They could not find a way over the Blue Mountains, west of Sydney. In 1813, John Blaxland, William Lawson and William Wentworth got through by climbing the mountain ridges instead of following the valleys.

Q **How did the explorers treat the Aborigines?**

A They assumed Europeans were superior and so had a right to take the Aborigines' land. The Aboriginal lifestyle was soon almost destroyed.

Many explorers relied on Aborigines to help them find food and water.

Who explored Africa?

Africa is a huge continent that was first explored by Europeans in the nineteenth century. Its deserts, rivers, plains and jungles were uncharted, making journeys difficult and dangerous.

Q Why was Africa so dangerous for explorers?

A Africa was such a wild place that it took very determined explorers to brave the hazards. They had to put up with disease, fierce animals, rugged surroundings and often hostile people.

Livingstone was once attacked by a lion, he survived but was badly injured.

Q Who found the source of the River Nile?

A The River Nile is the longest river in the world. It flows for 4,132 mi. through North Africa to the Mediterranean Sea. John Hanning Speke, a British explorer, discovered in 1862 that the Nile flowed out of Lake Victoria.

Q Who was the greatest explorer in Africa?

A The British explorer and missionary (spreader of Christianity) David Livingstone traveled nearly 31,070 mi. through Africa from 1841 until his death in 1873. He was missing in 1866 and was not found again until 1871. He was found by the American explorer Henry Morton Stanley who used the famous greeting: "Doctor Livingstone, I presume?"

The highest African mountain is Kilimanjaro (19,341 ft.) in Tanzania. A German, Hans Meyer, first reached the highest peak in 1889

Q Who was the most famous woman explorer of Africa?

A In the 1890s a British woman, Mary Kingsley, explored West Africa and discovered many unknown species of birds and animals. She also fought for justice and medical care for the African people.

Q Who explored the Sahara Desert?

A The Sahara is the largest desert in the world with an area of 3.5 million sq. mi. One-third of it is sand and the rest rocky wasteland. In the 1820s the Scottish explorers Hugh Clapperton and Walter Oudney, and English soldier Dixon Denham crossed the Sahara and made friends with Arab leaders.

Q What other great discoveries were made in Africa?

A The German explorer Heinrich Barth discovered the source of the Niger River in the 1850s and also discovered a new route across the Sahara Desert.

SAHARA
R. NIGER
R. NILE
Mt. KILIMANJARO

BARTH
STANLEY
LIVINGSTONE
SPEKE

On his journey to the North Pole, Robert Peary learned much from the Inuit (Eskimos) in his party.

ARCTIC OCEAN

NORTH
POLE

ALASKA

RUSSIA

GREENLAND

SOUTH
POLE
ANTARCTICA

The polar regions were only fully explored in the twentieth century. Polar exploration is still difficult today but modern technology has made the task less hazardous.

Q What are the differences between the North and the South Poles?

A The North Pole is in the frozen Arctic Ocean, which is surrounded by inhabited lands such as Greenland, Alaska and Canada. The South Pole is in Antarctica, which is a vast uninhabited area of frozen land surrounded by sea.

Q Who first reached the North Pole?

A In 1909 an American naval officer, Robert Peary, and his team, reached the North Pole with supplies pulled by a team of huskies. He suffered severe frostbite and lost all his toes.

Q Who first reached the South Pole?

A In 1911 the Norwegian Roald Amundsen reached the South Pole just one month ahead of the British naval officer Robert Falcon Scott, who reached the Pole in January, 1912. Scott and his four companions died during their return trip.

Q How did Amundsen beat Scott to the South Pole?

A Amundsen used dog teams (huskies) while Scott had ponies which could not stand the cold. Scott and his men ended up pulling their sledges themselves.

The boots of early polar explorers were sometimes stuffed with grass to keep their feet warm!

Q What did early polar explorers wear?

A Scott's team wore clothes made of cotton and wool which absorbed sweat, making them cold and wet. Amundsen's men wore furs and animal skins which let the body breathe as well as keeping it warm.

Q How do polar explorers keep warm today?

A They wear layers of clothes, trapping air between them. One layer is waterproof to stop sweat soaking outer layers of clothing. Outer clothes are windproof and padded.

Q What kind of shelters are needed?

A Tents are still used today but they are better insulated against the weather than those of the early explorers. Scientists working in polar regions for months at a time have proper buildings to work in.

Q What are the main dangers faced by polar explorers?

A Exposure (when the body is so chilled it cannot function) is the most serious hazard in polar cold. Frostbite, when the circulation of blood stops in fingers and toes, is another. Well-insulated clothes and warm food keep these at bay.

A search party found the bodies of Scott and his men in their tent eight months after they died.

What is a planet?

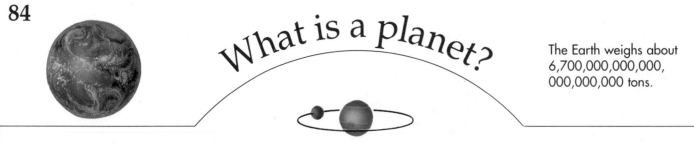

The Earth weighs about 6,700,000,000,000, 000,000,000 tons.

A planet is a world that travels around, or orbits, a star. Our planet - the Earth - orbits a star which we call the Sun. Both the Sun and the Earth are part of the Solar System.

Q What is the Solar System?

A It is a group of planets and about sixty moons in orbit around the Sun. The planets are Mercury, Venus, Earth, Mars, Jupiter, Saturn, Uranus, Neptune, and Pluto. Two newly discovered planets are called Smiley and Karla. There are also thousands of lumps of rock, called asteroids, which also orbit the Sun.

Q How was the Solar System formed?

A The Sun and its planets formed from a cloud of gas and dust whirling in space. The cloud was pulled together by gravity and it became very thick. Most of the cloud turned into what is now the Sun, and the rest made the planets, moons and asteroids.

Q Are there any other planets in space?

A The Solar System is a tiny part of a galaxy - the Milky Way - which contains 100 billion stars. The Milky Way is just one of more than ten billion galaxies in the Universe. It is almost certain that some other stars have planets, but they are hard to find because they are so far away. Scientists think they have found one about the same size as the Earth- it is about 186 million billion miles away.

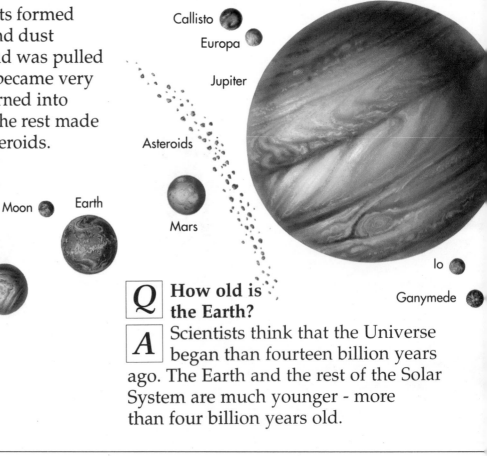

Callisto

Europa

Jupiter

Asteroids

Moon   Earth

Mars

Sun

Venus

Io

Mercury

Ganymede

Q How old is the Earth?

A Scientists think that the Universe began than fourteen billion years ago. The Earth and the rest of the Solar System are much younger - more than four billion years old.

The Milky Way is a good example of a spiral galaxy. It measures almost 70,000 light years across.

Q Why do we have day and night?

A The Earth gets light and heat from the Sun. As the Earth travels around the Sun, it also spins on its own axis (an imaginary line joining the North Pole, the center of the Earth and the South Pole). When your part of the Earth is facing the Sun you have daylight. When it turns away, darkness falls.

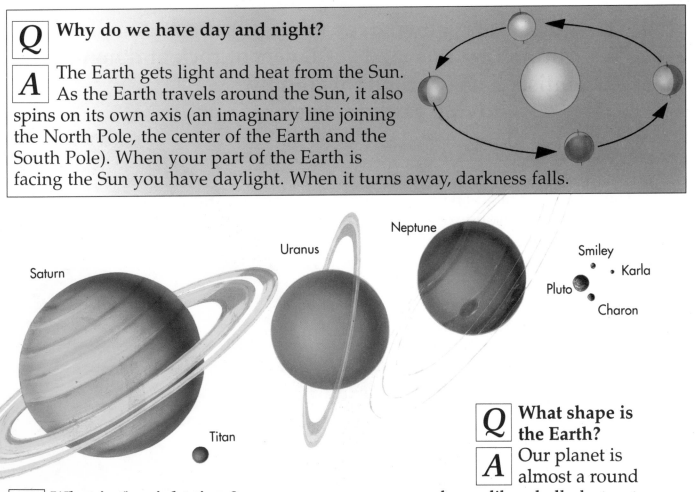

Saturn

Titan

Uranus

Neptune

Smiley

• Karla

Pluto

Charon

Q What is the right time?

A It depends where you are, because when it's day in one place it's night somewhere else. There are 24 time zones around the world. The time is different in each zone so you must reset your watch when you travel from one zone to another.

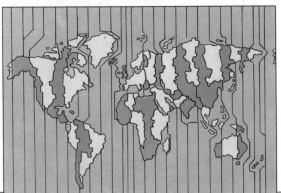

Q What shape is the Earth?

A Our planet is almost a round sphere - like a ball - but not quite. The speed at which the Earth spins causes the planet to bulge at the Equator and flatten at the Poles. This shape is called a spheroid.

Q If the Earth is spinning, why don't we fly off into space?

A We are held down by gravity. Everything "pulls" on everything else with a force - gravity. For most things gravity is too weak to notice, but the Earth is so large that it has a strong pull of gravity toward its center. The Sun's gravity is even stronger and it holds all the planets in orbit.

The temperature of the Earth's inner core is about 15,574°F.

The plates that make up the outer layers of the Earth move between 0.4 and 4 in. each year.

No one has dug down deep enough to be certain, but we think that it is made of layers of rock and metal. Scientists have worked this out by studying earthquakes.

Q What is inside the Earth?

A There are four main layers. The outer one is a layer of solid rock called the crust. Below this is the mantle. This is solid at the top, but deeper down it is so hot that the rocks have melted. Next is the outer core, made of hot liquid metal. At the center is the inner core, which is solid metal.

Crust

Mantle

Outer core

Inner core

Q Could we dig a tunnel to the other side of the Earth?

A No. The inner core of the Earth is far too hot. The deepest hole dug into the Earth is about 7.4 mi. deep.

Q Is the Earth magnetic?

A Yes, the Earth acts as though it has a huge bar magnet inside it, with a magnetic field and north and south poles. A compass needle points to the north magnetic pole. The Earth's magnetic field stretches thousands of miles into space.

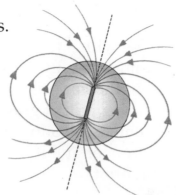

Q What is soil made of?

A There are many types of soil. They are all made of a mixture of pieces of rock, living particles, dead plant and animal material, air and water.

The Earth's crust is, on average, between 18.9 mi. and 24.8 mi. thick beneath the continents.

Under the oceans the crust is only 3-5 mi. thick.

150 million years ago

65 million years ago

180 million years ago

Today

Q Has the Earth always looked the same as it does now?

A No. The hard outer layers are split into large pieces, or plates. These plates have been moving very slowly for millions of years, and have moved the continents around.

Q How are rocks made?

A There are three types of rock on Earth and they are made in different ways. Igneous rocks are made when hot melted material, called magma, bubbles up from the mantle and hardens. Sedimentary rocks are layers of tiny pieces of other rocks, or dead plants and animals, which gradually build up and become cemented together. Metamorphic rocks are sedimentary or igneous rocks changed by great heat and pressure.

Q What makes earthquakes happen?

A Earthquakes occur when rocks move along faults, or cracks in the Earth's outer layers. Severe earthquakes happen when plates move past each other or toward each other. The rocks at the edges of the plates rub together, making the ground shake. Sometimes the plates "stick" for a while and pressure builds up. Then they break free suddenly, causing a huge earthquake.

Granite

Sandstone

Marble

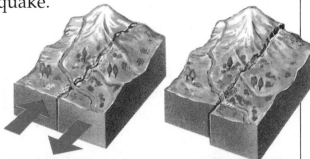

How many oceans are there?

Arctic

Pacific

Indian

Atlantic

The deepest scuba dive ever recorded was 452 ft. by John J. Gruener and R. Neal Watson.

There are four large oceans on Earth - the Pacific, the Atlantic, the Indian and the Arctic. There are also smaller areas of water called seas. Most seas are actually part of the oceans or are joined on to them.

Q How big are the oceans?

A Oceans and seas cover about seven-tenths of the Earth's surface. The Pacific is the largest ocean, with an area of about 64 million sq. mi., followed by the Atlantic, with about 31 million sq mi., and the Indian, at about 28 million sq. mi. The Arctic Ocean is the smallest at about 4.6 million sq. mi.

Arctic
Indian
Atlantic
Pacific

Q How were the oceans formed?

A No one is certain. Some scientists think that soon after the Earth was formed it was surrounded by thick clouds. As the Earth cooled down, rain fell and filled the hollows in the crust to form the first oceans. When the continents drifted apart, water filled the gaps they left to form the modern oceans we know today.

Q Why is seawater salty?

A The salty taste of seawater comes from minerals that have been washed into the sea by rivers. The most common mineral is salt.

Q What makes waves?

A Waves are made by wind blowing across the surface of the water. The wind pushes the water upward, making a wave crest, and then gravity pulls it back down again, into a wave trough.

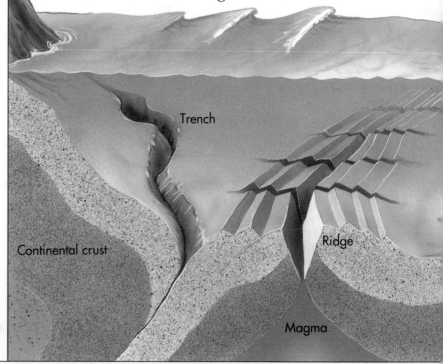

Trench

Continental crust

Ridge

Magma

Seawater contains gold - about 4 grams in every million tons of water. It also contains silver, calcium and sulphur.

The biggest wave ever recorded in the open sea was seen from a ship during a storm in 1933. It was 111 ft. high!

Q How does a coral reef grow?

A Coral reefs form in warm, shallow waters. They are made by tiny animals called polyps, which have hard, cup-shaped shells. Thousands of polyps live side by side and their shells join together to form a reef. When the polyps die, their hard shells remain. More polyps grow on top of them and gradually the reef grows.

Q How are islands formed?

A Some islands are areas of land that were joined to continents long ago when the sea level was lower than it is now. The British Isles, for example, were once connected to mainland Europe. Other islands are the tops of volcanoes that rise up from the seabed. The island of Surtsey, near Iceland, was formed in this way. Between November, 1963 and June, 1967, the island rose more than 948 ft. from the ocean floor, leaving it 558 ft. above sea level.

Volcanic island

Q Is the bottom of the ocean flat?

A No. The ocean floor has many hills, valleys, deep trenches and high mountain ranges. The Mid-Atlantic Ridge, which runs for 12,428 mi. down the center of the Atlantic Ocean, is the longest mountain range in the world. The deepest point is the Marianas Trench, in the Pacific Ocean which plunges to 36,199 ft. below sea level.

Oceanic crust

90

Every 100 years, the level of the sea rises by about 12 in.

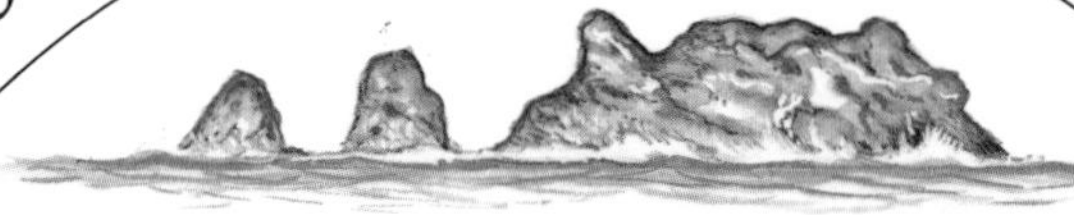

Waves can erode cliffs to form weird shapes. These different shapes are given special names.

Coastlines are where the land meets the sea. There are many different types of coastline, ranging from sandy beaches to rocky cliffs. They are all shaped by the sea.

Q Do coastlines always stay the same shape?

A No, they are always changing. Some coastlines are being worn away by the pounding of the sea. In other places, beaches are being made.

Q Is the sand on beaches always yellow?

A No, not always. Yellow sand consists mainly of a mineral called quartz. In the Hawaiian Islands, the sand is black because it is made from black lava produced by erupting volcanoes.

Cave

Direction of waves

Q How does the sea wear away the land?

A Waves do most of the wearing away, or eroding, of coastlines. As waves approach the coast, they pick up sand, pebbles and larger pieces of rock from the sea floor and, during storms, hurl them against the shore, breaking off more pieces of rock.

Stack

Durdle Dor in England is a good example of an arch.

A stack is a single column of rock. The Old Man of Hoy in the Orkney Islands is a famous example of a stack.

Q How are beaches made?

A Beaches form along stretches of coast that are sheltered from strong waves, such as in bays. Most beach sand is brought from inland by rivers flowing into the sea. Some is made when rocks broken off by the sea are worn down into smaller and smaller pieces. Sand is dropped along the shore by waves and it builds up into beaches.

Q Can we take back land from the sea?

A Yes. Coastal marshes and even shallow bays can be reclaimed from the sea. The first step is usually to build a protective wall to stop the sea flooding the area. Then the salt water is drained or pumped out, leaving dry land.

Protective wall

Beach

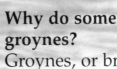

Groynes

Q Why do some beaches have groynes?

A Groynes, or breakwaters, are built stretching into the sea to stop beaches from being worn away by waves.

Q What causes high and low tides?

A Tides rise and fall twice in every 24 hours and 50 minutes. They are caused mainly by the Moon. When the Moon is overhead, its gravity pulls upward on the sea, away from the shore, causing a bulge like a large wave. This is low tide. As the Earth spins, the wave travels around the planet, causing high tides.

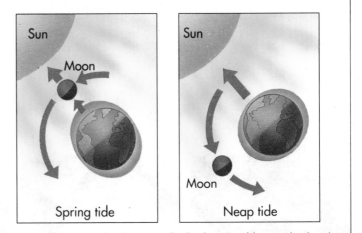

Sun
Moon
Spring tide

Sun
Moon
Neap tide

Spring and neap tides occur twice a month. They are the highest and lowest high tides.

These are the five highest mountains in the world.

Mount Everest 29,030 ft.

Have there always been mountains?

The first mountains may have been made soon after the Earth was formed, but they were worn away many millions of years ago. The mountains we can see today are much younger.

Q Where are the world's highest mountains?

A The world's 20 highest mountains (measured from sea level) are all in the Himalaya-Karakoram range in Asia. Mount Everest is the tallest at 29,030 ft. The highest mountain from top to bottom is the peak of Mauna Kea in the Hawaiian Islands. It rises 33,476 ft. from the ocean floor, but as over half of it is underwater only 13,797 ft. rises above sea level.

Q Do mountains always stay the same?

A No. Mountains are being worn away by rain, wind, frost and other natural forces. Some mountain ranges, such as the Alps, Himalayas and Andes, are still rising as the continental plates they rest on are pushed closer together.

Q What is a rift valley?

A Where two faults run side by side, the block of land between them may sink down to form a rift valley. The most famous example is the Great Rift Valley which runs for 3,977 mi. from Syria down through East Africa.

Q How are mountains made?

A Some mountains are volcanoes. Others are dome mountains which were pushed up by hot melted, or molten, rock rising below the surface. Some mountains formed when rocks were squeezed together and folded. Others are blocks of land forced up between huge cracks, or faults, in the Earth's surface.

Volcanic   Dome   Folds   Fault

K2
28,709 ft.

Kangchenjunga
28,207 ft.

Lhotse
27,924 ft.

Makalu I
27,826 ft.

Q Why do high mountains have snow on top?

A For every 3,200 ft. that you go up, the temperature of the air falls by about 13°F. The tops of high mountains are always surrounded by very cold air, even in summer.

Q What is a volcano?

A A volcano is a hole in the Earth's crust. When a volcano erupts, hot molten rocks from inside the Earth pour out of the hole on to the surface. Volcanoes that erupt often are called active, while those that might erupt some time in the future are said to be dormant. A volcano that has stopped erupting is said to be extinct.

Q Where are there volcanoes?

A There are about 1,300 active volcanoes (ones that erupt) in the world, although only about twenty to thirty erupt in any one year. Most volcanoes are in areas near the edges of the plates which make up the Earth's outer layers.

Active volcanoes around the world.

The deepest lake is Lake Baikal, in Russia, which is 6,365 ft. deep.

How are rivers made?

The water in rivers comes from rain, lakes, springs and melting ice and snow. Rivers often begin high up on mountains and run downhill to the sea. As they flow, they wear away the land to make valleys.

Q Why do rivers get larger as they flow?

A A river usually starts as a tiny trickle called a rill. It flows downhill and is joined by other rills. It gets larger and becomes a stream. Other streams flow into it to make a river. A river may have other rivers, called tributaries, flowing into it and so it gets bigger and bigger.

Q Which is the world's longest river?

A The Nile is the longest, at 4,160 mi. It flows through East Africa into the Mediterranean Sea. The river that contains the most water is the Amazon in South America. Every second it carries about 4,237,680 cu. ft. of water into the Atlantic Ocean.

Tributary

Delta

Lake

Q How is a delta formed?

A As a river rushes downhill, it washes with it mud, sand and even boulders from its bed and banks. As the river approaches the sea, it flows over flat land and slows down, dropping the material. If tides don't wash away the sand and mud, it builds up to form new land, called a delta.

The world's largest freshwater lake is Lake Superior. It covers an area of 31,660 sq. mi. in the U.S. and Canada.

Each year the Huang He, or Yellow River, in China washes about 2,240 million tons of soil down its valley.

Q How are lakes formed?

A Most of the world's lakes are in places where glaciers carved out deep valleys in the land (see pages 18-19). Some lakes, such as Lake Tanganyika in Africa, are in deep valleys called rift valleys, which are made by huge movements in the Earth's crust. A lake may form in the craters of volcanoes, or when a river changes its course.

Q Why don't rivers run straight?

A On their way downhill to the sea, rivers travel along the easiest routes. If a river meets something in its way, such as a boulder or a hill, it simply flows around it.

Waterfall

Stream

Cave

Underground river

Q Are there rivers under the ground?

A Yes, especially in areas where there is limestone. Rainwater can wear away limestone, making holes and caves. A river on the surface may pour down a hole in the rock and flow through the caves underground.

Q How are waterfalls made?

A Most waterfalls form where a river flows over a layer of hard rock and then over softer rock. The river wears away the softer rock faster than the hard rock, making a step. The step gradually gets deeper and the river plunges over it, creating a waterfall.

Many plants and animals have adapted to living in the deserts.

Are all deserts hot and sandy?

The saguaro cactus can grow up to 50 ft. high.

An area is called desert if, on average, it has less than ten inches of rain a year. Deserts are often in hot places, but not always. Most deserts are covered with rocks and stones rather than sand.

Q Where are the world's deserts?

A The world's largest deserts are in regions with high air pressure. Winds blow outward from these areas and moist winds from the sea very rarely blow into them. Other deserts are far from the sea. By the time winds reach them, they have lost most of their moisture. Some deserts are on the inland, sheltered sides of mountain ranges. Most of Antarctica is a frozen desert. It is a region of high pressure and little new snow falls inland.

Q Which is the world's driest desert?

A Many deserts go without rain for several years at a time and then have a short downpour. The driest desert is the Atacama in South America; until 1971, it had not rained there for four hundred years.

Q What is an oasis?

A An oasis is an area of land in a desert where plants are able to grow because there is water from an underground spring or a well.

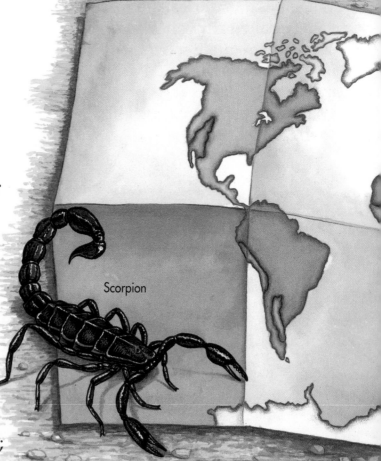

Scorpion

Q How do sand dunes move?

A Wind blows loose sand along the ground and piles it up into hills called dunes. Sand grains are blown up one side of a dune and rolled over the top and down the steep face on the other side. Sand grains are always being blown up and over the dune, moving it across the desert.

Dromedary

Cholla

Ocetillo

Kangaroo rat

Q Which is the largest desert?

A The Sahara desert, in North Africa, is the biggest. It covers an area of about 3,243,240 sq. mi. Only about a tenth of it is covered with sand; the rest is rocky.

The World's deserts

Hot desert

Polar desert

Cactus

Q Can plants and animals live in the desert?

A Yes. Plants and animals have developed special ways of living in deserts. Some plant seeds stay buried in the sand for years until it rains. Then they grow quickly and produce seeds of their own before dying off when the sand dries out. Most desert animals hide during the day and come out at night when it is cooler. Some can store water in their bodies for a long time.

Rattlesnake

Gila monster

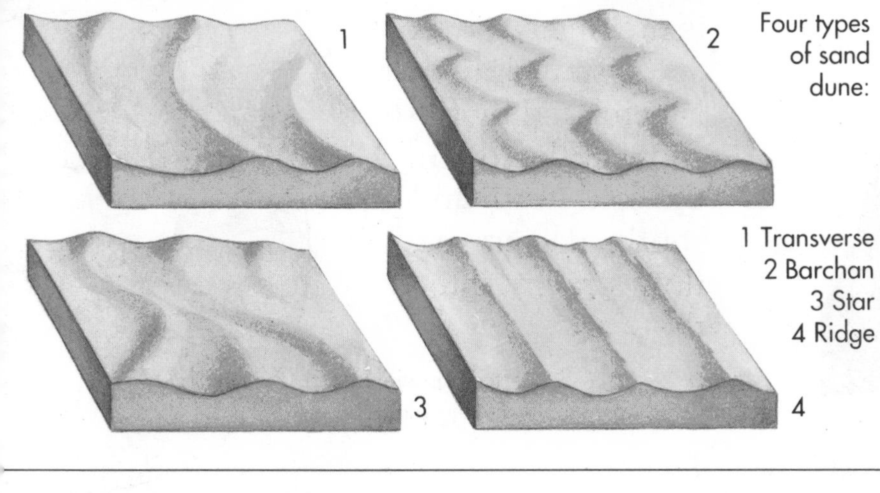

Four types of sand dune:

1 Transverse
2 Barchan
3 Star
4 Ridge

1

2

3

4

Q Do deserts change size?

A Sometimes they grow and at other times they shrink. In 1987 the Sahara spread 33 mi. south in one area, but the following year it retreated 60 mi. north.

What is a glacier?

A glacier is like a river of ice. It forms when snow piles up in a hollow on a mountainside. As the snow continues to build up it gets squeezed together turning into ice. Finally, the ice spills out of the hollow and flows slowly downhill as a glacier.

Q What is an ice age?

A An ice age is a period in which temperatures are much lower than normal and ice sheets spread across large parts of the Earth. Ice ages happen every few million years. The most recent one ended about ten thousand years ago. Parts of North America and Europe were covered by ice sheets.

Q How thick is an ice sheet?

A The ice sheets that covered much of North America and Europe during the last ice age were up to 9,800 ft. thick. The ice covering the continent of Antarctica today is even thicker - 15,740 ft. in places.

A cross-section through an ice sheet.

Q Are there any glaciers in the world today?

A Yes. There are glaciers in the cold lands at the far north and south of the Earth, in northern Canada, Greenland and Antarctica, for example. Glaciers also slide down valleys in high mountain ranges, such as the Himalayas, the Rockies and the Alps.

Q Why do glaciers stop moving?

A As a glacier slides down a mountain it moves into warmer regions and begins to melt. Eventually it gets to a point where it is melting at the bottom at the same rate that it is being fed by fresh snow at the top. In the cold north and south, glaciers may flow straight into the sea.

A close-up view of a melting glacier.

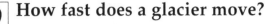

The deep sea inlets, or fjords, along the coasts of Scandinavia were made by glaciers.

Q How fast does a glacier move?

A Most glaciers move downhill quite slowly, at less than 12 in. a day. The Quaraya Glacier in Greenland is much quicker, speeding along at around 79 ft. a day. Some glaciers have short bursts of energy during which they race down at up to 390 ft. a day. These bursts last for a few months and then the glacier slows down again.

Q What do glaciers and ice sheets do to the land?

A They wear away, or erode, the land they move over. The ice pulls pieces of rock from the land beneath it. Rocks fall on to the ice from above. All of these pieces of rock become frozen into the ice. As the glacier or ice sheet moves, the rocks grind against the land, wearing it away. When the ice melts, the rocks are dropped on the ground. These rocks are called moraine.

Q Where are the longest glaciers in the world?

A Most are in Antarctica, including the longest of all - the Lambert-Fisher Ice Passage which is 320 mi. in length.

Where are the polar regions?

Antarctica contains ninety percent of the world's ice.

The polar regions are at the far north and south of the Earth. The Arctic lies inside the Arctic Circle, an imaginary line around the North Pole. The Antarctic is a continent that surrounds the South Pole.

Arctic circle

North Pole

Arctic wildlife

Q How much of the world is covered with ice?

A Ice covers more than one-tenth of the Earth's land surface. The Greenland ice sheet covers about 695,000 sq. mi. while the ice sheet in Antarctica is over 5,000,000 sq. mi. About three-quarters of all the world's fresh water is frozen in ice sheets and glaciers.

Q What are the North and South Poles?

A The Poles are the places on the Earth which are farthest north and south. If you stood at the North Pole, which ever way you walked you would be going south.

Q What is underneath the polar ice?

A Beneath the ice in Antarctica lies a vast continent, with high mountains and deep valleys. The ice around the North Pole in the Arctic is not resting on land but simply floating on the sea.

Here are three of the many different shapes of iceberg that can be found at the Poles.

Slab   Jagged   Pyramidal

Q | What is an iceberg?

A | Where ice sheets and glaciers flow down into the sea, huge chunks of ice - icebergs - can break off and float away. The tallest one ever seen stood 548 ft. above the water and extended more than a mile below the surface. The largest iceberg ever seen was near Antarctica in 1956. It covered an area of more than 11,970 sq. mi.

Q | Which is colder, the Arctic or the Antarctic?

A | The Antarctic gets far colder than the Arctic. The coldest place of all is the Vostok Base in Antarctica, close to the South Pole. In July, 1983, an air temperature of -243.7°F was recorded there.

Q | Is it always snowing in the Antarctic?

A | No, the Antarctic actually gets very little snow, especially in the center. The air over the continent is very cold and also very dry, and only about 2 in. of snow falls in a year. Close to the coasts, where it is not so cold and there is more moisture in the air, much more snow falls.

Q | Does anyone live in Antarctica?

A | No one lives there permanently. There are a number of research stations where scientists live for months at a time and study the area. Away from the coast, Antarctica has almost no life at all other than one type of tiny mite, several mosses and two species of flowering plant.

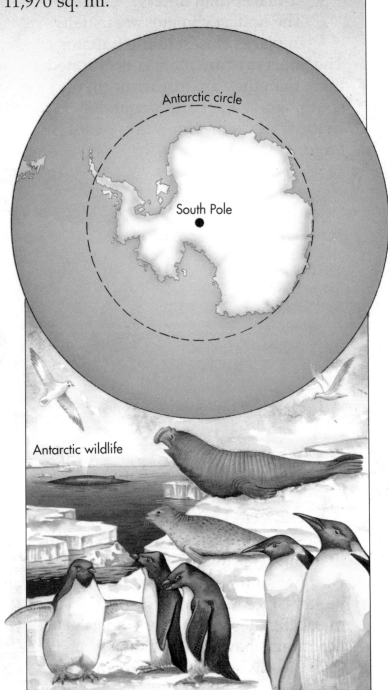

Antarctic circle

South Pole

Antarctic wildlife

What is climate?

Siberia, in Russia, has the greatest range of temperatures during a year, from -191°F to 102°F.

The type of weather that a place usually has from year to year is called its climate. Some places are warm all year round while others are always very cold. In some areas the temperature changes from season to season.

Q Why do some places have hotter climates than others?

A The hottest climates are usually in places closest to the Equator. The Sun's rays are more concentrated there than they are further north or south, where the Earth's rounded shape spreads the Sun's rays over a larger area.

Q How many types of climate are there?

A The world is divided into four main types of climate: polar, temperate, subtropical and tropical. Some areas, such as deserts and mountains, have their own special types of climate.

Map showing vegetation regions

Q What things can affect climate?

A The climate of a particular place is affected by a number of things. Places near the sea have milder climates than those far inland, which often have very hot summers and freezing winters. Ocean currents can make climates warmer or colder. Mountains have colder climates than the lowlands around them.

Q Do cities have their own climates?

A Yes, cities are often warmer than the surrounding areas. Concrete buildings absorb heat from the Sun during the day and release it at night, making the air in the city warmer.

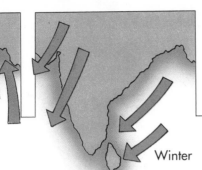

Summer | Winter

The seasons come at different times of the year in different places.

When it is summer in Europe it is winter in Australia.

Q What is a monsoon?

A A monsoon is a type of wind. In some places near the Equator, air over the land heats up in summer and rises. Cool, wet air from the ocean blows in to take its place, bringing heavy rain. In winter the winds reverse and dry air blows from the land towards the sea.

Q Does climate affect which plants grow where?

A Yes. Different types of plant prefer different climates. For example, rainforests grow in the hot, wet areas around the Equator, and coniferous forests grow in the cold areas in the north. Farther north, where it is even colder, only mosses and tiny flowers can survive.

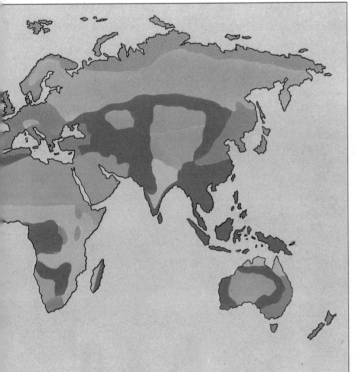

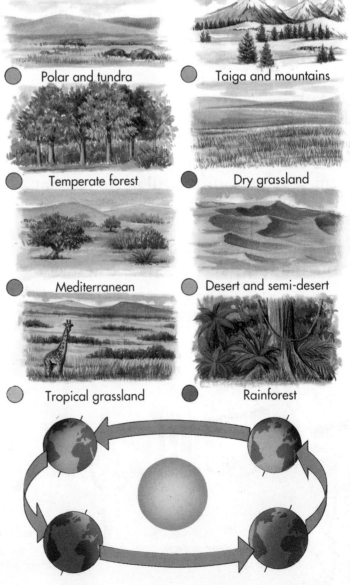

Polar and tundra
Taiga and mountains
Temperate forest
Dry grassland
Mediterranean
Desert and semi-desert
Tropical grassland
Rainforest

Q Why do we have seasons?

A As the Earth moves around the Sun, different parts of it are tilted towards the Sun for a few months at a time. The part leaning towards the Sun has summer, while the part leaning away has winter.

More than 20 percent of the world's oil comes from the rocks beneath the sea.

What are the Earth's natural resources?

The first large scale nuclear plant was built in 1956.

Almost everything we use, such as the fuel we burn, the wood and stone we use for building and the food we eat, comes from the Earth in some way. These things are called natural resources.

Q What are fossil fuels?

A They are fuels, such as coal, oil and gas, that were formed from the remains of animals and plants that lived and died millions of years ago.

Q What are renewable energy sources?

A When fossil fuels are used they can't be renewed, or made again. Some energy sources will never run out. They are called renewable sources and include running water, the wind, energy from the Sun and even heat from the rocks deep inside the Earth.

Q How is nuclear power produced?

A Everything in the Universe is made of tiny particles, called atoms. When atoms are broken apart they give off heat, which can be used to produce electricity. This is done inside nuclear power stations. The atoms most often used are uranium.

Hydroelectric dams produce electricity from running water.

Solar panels store energy from the sun

Wind turbines use the wind to produce electricity.

Geothermal plants use energy from rocks below the ground.

There are about 70,000 different varieties of rice in the world.

Q Which food crops are the most important?

A Cereals, or grain crops, are used to feed more people in the world than any other type. Rice and wheat are the most important grain crops.

Q What are staple foods?

A Your staple food is the one that you eat most often. In Asia, for example, people eat more rice than anything else. Staple foods in Europe and North America include bread, potatoes and pasta.

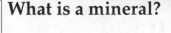

Q What is a mineral?

A Minerals are natural, non-living substances that are found in the Earth. There are about 3,000 types of mineral, each made from its own special combination of atoms. Some minerals, such as diamonds, rubies and emeralds are very rare and valuable. Others, like quartz, are extremely common.

Copper

Quartz

Ruby

Diamond

How many fish can be caught in one go?

In 1986 a Norwegian fishing boat hauled in a single catch weighing more than 2,300 tons. It was estimated to contain about 120 million fish.

Q Do the oceans have resources?

A Yes. The rocks of the sea-bed contain minerals, including oil and gas, and metals. We catch fish to eat in the oceans, and the seawater itself can be made into water for drinking. Waves and tides are also renewable energy sources.

Are we damaging the planet?

We are damaging the Earth in a number of ways - by polluting the air, soil and water, by destroying the places where plants and animals live, and by using up its natural resources.

Q What is pollution?

A Pollution means spoiling our environment by putting into the air, water or land materials that will harm it. Humans have always polluted the planet with smoke, trash and other things. Pollution is now very serious because there are many more humans than ever before.

Q What is global warming?

A Some gases in the atmosphere, such as carbon dioxide, help to trap in heat from the Sun. Factories, cars and power stations produce a lot more of these gases, and so more heat is being trapped in. If the Earth keeps getting warmer, the Antarctic ice sheet may begin to melt and the sea level would rise, flooding some low coasts.

Q Where does our trash go?

A Some is burned, which causes air pollution and adds to global warming. Most is either buried in holes in the ground or dumped at sea, causing more pollution. Little is reused or recycled, even though glass, metals, paper and plastics can all be treated and reused.

There are between five and eight million different species of plants and animals in the world. So far, only 1.6 million have been identified and many of the rest may become extinct even before we discover them.

Q How does rain become acid?

A All rainwater is very slightly acidic. When fossil fuels are burned - in car engines, factories and power stations - chemicals are produced which make the moisture in the air much more acidic. Eventually, this moisture falls to the ground as acid rain.

Q Are there holes in the ozone layer?

A The ozone layer protects us from harmful ultraviolet radiation from the Sun. The ozone is being destroyed by chemicals called CFCs, which are used in aerosol cans, coolants, and some plastics. So far, there aren't any actual holes in the ozone layer, but it has become thin in places. Many countries have now stopped using CFCs.

A satellite view of the ozone layer. The pink color shows the thin areas.

Q Why do people cut down rainforests?

A The world's tropical rainforests are cut down to make grazing land for cattle and to use certain hardwood trees for making furniture. The forests are being destroyed at a rate of about 9 sq. mi. every hour. If this continues, by the year 2050 there will be none left.

Q Does recycling paper save rainforests?

A No, because the trees used for making paper are specially grown. Recycling paper makes sense because it uses far less energy and water than making new paper from trees. It also means that we throw less away, which reduces pollution.

When the sea was first formed it was hot, only a few degrees below boiling point, and as acidic as lemon juice!

What do we know about the sea?

The sea covers two-thirds of the Earth and contains 97 percent of all its water. As well as being the home of millions of fascinating creatures, humans rely on it for food, energy and fun.

Q What is the sea made of?

A The sea is made of saltwater that contains every natural element known on Earth - altogether more than 100! If you dissolved a teaspoon of table salt in a glass of water, this would show you how salty the sea is. Sodium and chlorine, the main components of table salt, make up 85 percent of the dissolved salts in seawater. Seawater also contains calcium, magnesium and even traces of arsenic and gold!

Q Why is the sea blue?

A The sea is blue because it reflects the color of the sky. When a cloud is overhead you can see it cast a shadow on the sea. The color can also depend on how deep the water is. From above shallow water with sand on the seabed tends to look paler blue than deeper water with dark seaweed on the bottom. Weather conditions can also change the look of the sea. It can look dark gray in a storm.

Q Can sound travel through seawater?

A Yes. However, sound travels through sea water 4.5 times faster than it does through air. Because of this it is hard to tell what direction sound is coming from underwater as it seems to reach both ears at the same time.

The sea is a layer of water with an average depth of 2.3 miles on the surface of a sphere 800 miles wide.

There is enough salt in the sea to cover the land with a layer 500 ft. thick.

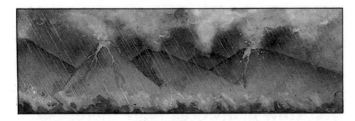

Q How was the sea first formed?

A Although they cannot be sure, scientists believe that the oceans were formed by massive clouds of water vapor rising from volcanoes and hot rocks on the Earth's surface not long after it was formed. As the surface cooled, the water vapor turned to rain which fell and fell, gradually filling up dips in the Earth's surface and taking with it any mineral salts on the land... and so forming the saltwater oceans.

Q Where does seawater come from?

A Very little new water is ever made on Earth. It is just the same supply used over and over again. As the sun heats up the sea, millions of gallons of water rise up into the air as invisible water vapor. Clouds form as the water vapor cools, then as they drift over the land it rains or snows. Rivers collect the water and carry it straight back into the sea, and the whole process begins again. This is called the water cycle.

Q Can light travel through seawater?

A Sunlight is made up of the same colors you can see in a rainbow, starting with red and ending in violet. Each color can only travel to a certain depth in seawater. For instance, red light fades out first at around 16 feet whereas violet light can go as deep as 250 feet. Brightly colored fish look dull if you see them deep down.

The hottest seawater is in the Persian Gulf. In summer the surface temperature can reach 97.3°F!

What is an ocean?

An ocean is a large body of water which is joined to other oceans and seas. Together they form one big stretch of water that flows continually around the world.

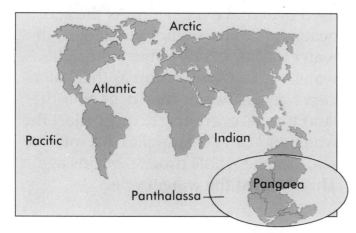

Arctic

Atlantic

Pacific

Indian

Panthalassa — Pangaea

Q **How many oceans are there?**

A Today there are four recognized oceans. They are the Pacific, the Atlantic, the Indian and the Arctic. About 170 million years ago all the continents formed one piece of land called Pangaea. Surrounding it was one vast ocean called Panthalassa. As Pangaea slowly split into today's seven continents, Panthalassa became the four oceans.

Q **Which is the deepest ocean?**

A The Pacific Ocean is the deepest as well as the largest. The deepest point in the ocean, and on Earth, is Marianas Trench, at 36,202 ft. Mount Everest, the highest mountain on Earth at 29,030 ft., could be sunk without trace into it. If a boat were to drop a 2 lb. steel anchor over the side it would take over an hour to reach the bottom of the trench!

Q **What is the difference between an ocean and a sea?**

A Oceans are bigger than seas. Some seas are parts of oceans, such as the Arabian Sea in the Indian Ocean. Other seas are enclosed by land, such as the Caspian Sea in Asia. All the oceans together are often just called "the sea."

Fossilized sea shells found on Mount Everest show that the Himalayas were once part of the sea floor. Changes in the Earth's crust pushed them up into the air about forty million years ago.

Only one-ninth of an iceberg is ever visible above the sea's surface.

Q Which is the largest ocean?

A The Pacific is the largest ocean, covering one third of the Earth. At its widest point, the Pacific measures 11,000 miles, stretching nearly halfway around the world!

Q Which is the coldest ocean?

A The Arctic is the coldest ocean as well as the smallest. For most of the year it is frozen solid. In some places the ice measures up to 1 mile thick! The Arctic Ocean is dotted with thousands of icebergs, with up to 15,000 new ones being formed each year!

Q In which ocean is the saltiest sea?

A The Red Sea in the Indian Ocean has the saltiest sea water in the world. Part of it, known as the Dead Sea, is famous for people being able to float on its surface with no effort at all. It is called the Dead Sea because nothing can live in the salty water.

Q Which is the smallest ocean?

A The Arctic Ocean is the smallest ocean, covering an area of 4,732,428 sq. mi.

Q Which is the warmest ocean?

A The Indian Ocean holds the record for being the warmest ocean. The temperature of the surface water can reach 97.3°F! It is the third largest ocean covering an area of 28,416,960 sq. mi.

The greatest tides occur in the Bay of Fundy in Canada, where they can rise to over 50 ft. high.

What are currents and tides?

The waters of the world's oceans and seas are continually flowing. They are moved by the wind, waves, tides and currents.

Q What is a current?

A Currents are bodies of water that always flow in the same direction. They are driven mainly by the wind.

Q What is the Gulf Stream?

A The Gulf Stream is one of the strongest, warmest and saltiest currents. It runs along the east coast of the United States, separating the warm, salty Sargasso Sea from the cold, less salty inshore water.

Westerlies

Trade Winds

Q What causes a current?

A Wind-driven currents are controlled by two types of winds. These are called the Westerlies (that blow from west to east), and the Trade Winds (that blow from east to west). These winds force the warm water at the Equator out toward the cold water of the North Pole in a clockwise direction, and out toward the cold water of the South Pole in a counter clockwise direction.

Low tide

High tide

Q What are tides?

A Tides are the sea level rising and falling twice each day. You can see the tide is rising when the water covers the beach. When the water stops rising it is high tide. The water level then falls back until low tide is reached.

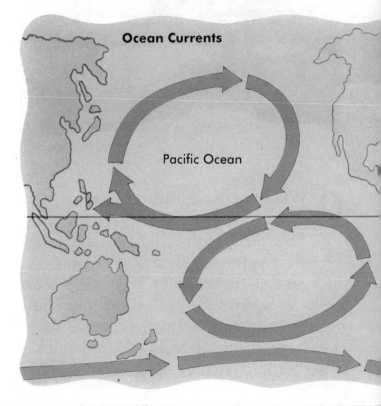
Ocean Currents

Pacific Ocean

Warm currents may be as hot as 82°F, while cold currents may be as cold as -5.5°F.

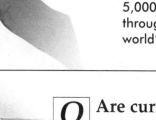

One drop of sea water may take 5,000 years to travel through all the world's oceans.

Q Are currents dangerous?

A Yes. Underwater sea currents cause many deaths each year. Bathers swim out to areas which look calm on the surface, but then they are pulled away from or along the shore by strong currents underneath. Once trapped in the pull of a current, a swimmer can become exhausted and even drown.

Q What causes high and low tides?

A Tides are caused by the Moon's gravity pulling the Earth's oceans into two bulges, one facing the Moon and another on the other side of the planet. As the Moon travels around the Earth, it drags these bulges of water with it. As the bulge hits the land, the water piles up, creating a high tide. Between the bulges the water is lower, creating a low tide.

Earth   Moon

Q What causes spring and neap tides?

A When the Moon is lined up with the Sun, they pull together on the same point of the Earth's surface. This big pull causes a massive bulge which makes the high tides very high and the low tides very low. This is known as a spring tide. When the Moon has moved to a right angle with the Sun, their pull evens out and so there is no bulge.

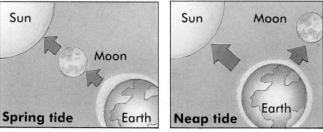

Sun   Moon
Moon
Spring tide   Earth   **Neap tide**   Earth

During this time there is very little difference between low and high tide. This is called a neap tide. A spring and a neap tide occur twice a month.

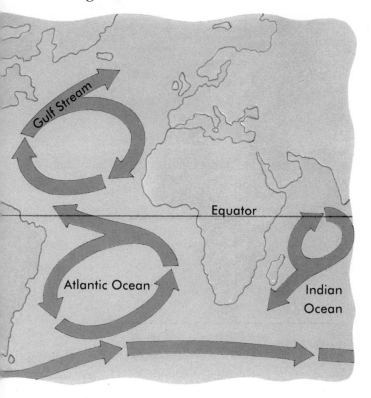

Gulf Stream

Equator

Atlantic Ocean

Indian Ocean

The largest tsunami ever recorded was off the Japanese coast in 1971. It was 279 ft. high!

How are waves formed?

Waves come in all shapes and sizes, from small and rippling to huge and crashing. Some can even capsize a ship.

 Q What is a wave?

A A wave is a mass of tiny water particles going around in a circular movement. Each water droplet ends up exactly where it began in the circle.

Q What makes waves?

A Waves are made by the wind blowing across the surface of the water. The wind pushes the water upward and then gravity pulls it back down again. So the stronger the wind and the longer it blows, the bigger the waves it creates.

Q What are tidal waves, or tsunamis?

A They are giant waves caused by earthquakes and volcanic eruptions under the sea. They explode on the shore causing great damage, and can even drown whole islands.

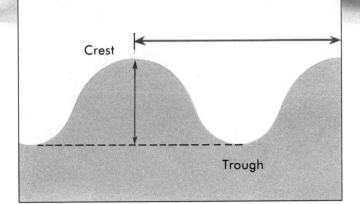

 Q How do you measure a wave?

A To see how big a wave is, you have to measure from its crest (the highest point of the wave) to its trough (the lowest point of the wave).

Crest

Trough

In June 1968, the tanker World Glory was broken in two by a series of 100 foot-high waves.

The white foam that forms on the crests of waves is often called "white horses."

Q **Are waves dangerous?**

A Some waves can be very dangerous, especially in storms. They can wreck ships out at sea. Freak waves sometimes rise up and snatch people from the shore, dragging them into the sea. Surfers often try to ride extremely high waves, which can crush and drown them if they fall off their surfboards.

Q **What height can waves reach?**

A Waves can reach enormous heights. The highest natural wave ever recorded was 112 ft., seen from *USS Ramapo* during a storm in the Pacific Ocean in 1933. That is over twenty times taller than an average person!

Q **What are waterspouts?**

A Waterspouts are enormous columns of water drawn up by the wind quite suddenly. In the Gulf of Mexico, winds blowing at up to 600 mph turn into tornadoes or whirlwinds as they come off the land and whip up massive waterspouts. Some may be 32 ft. thick and 390 ft. high!

Not all beaches have yellow sand. Hawaiian beaches have black sand, formed from volcanic lava.

What is on the seashore?

The seashore is where the land meets the sea. Some seashores have flat beaches, while others have steep cliffs. They are always busy with all kinds of wildlife.

Q How are beaches made?

A Rocks are constantly broken off from the land by the sea and worn down into smaller and smaller pieces, making pebbles or sand. These are then dropped off along the shore by waves and a beach is gradually formed. Sand is also brought from inland by rivers flowing into the sea.

Q What lives under the sand on a beach?

A Sandy beaches may not seem to have many creatures living on them at first glance. But if you look carefully you will see signs of life. Tiny holes, hollows and piles of coiled sand give away the hiding places of bristle worms, rag worms, cockles and burrowing starfish and crabs. Under the sand they are protected from the Sun, predators and tides.

Q How does the sea shape the seashore?

A Waves are constantly wearing away the shore and changing its shape. It hollows out caves and arches in cliffs.

Q What plants do you find on the seashore?

A Algae and seaweed are the only plants you find on the seashore. Most plants do not like salt water and sea breezes.

Like rocks, seaweeds provide a cool hiding place for creatures while they wait for the tide to come in. Gently turn clumps of seaweed over and see what is hiding underneath!

Cockle

Fan worm

Sand gaper

Razor shell

Winkle

Mussel

Shrimp

Lugworm

The Bermuda Islands have pale pink beaches. The sand is made from tiny pieces of red shell.

The dazzling white beaches of Barbados are made from tiny pieces of white shell.

Sometimes arches collapse leaving rock stacks.

Groynes, or breakwaters, are built on some beaches to stop the sand or pebbles from being dragged away by the sea.

Q What is a strandline?

A When the tide comes in it leaves behind a long line of debris at its edge. It is called a strandline. People go beachcombing along strandlines, searching for pretty seashells, mermaid's purses (shark's egg cases), crab shells, cuttlefish bones, driftwood and even useful trash.

Q What animals like beaches?

A Sea birds, such as gulls, feed on dead fish and crabs washed up on the strandline. Wading birds use their long beaks for finding worms in the sand. Huge colonies of seals gather on beaches at certain times of the year to mate.

Oystercatcher

Seagull

Limpet

Welk

Blenny

Anemone

Starfish

Crab

Hermit crab

Q What might you find in a rock pool?

A Water is trapped in the hollows of rocks (worn out of them by the sea) when the tide goes out, forming rock pools. They provide a home for many creatures. Starfish, anemones, limpets, periwinkles and muscles cling to the rocks, while shrimp, crabs and different types of fish shelter underneath them.

Many flatfish can change their skin color and pattern to match whatever surface they rest on.

What lives in the sea?

Life on Earth started in the sea over 3,500 million years ago. At one time almost all life existed there. Today, there is still a bigger variety of animal and plant life in the sea than on land.

Q What is plankton?

A Plankton is a soup of millions of tiny plants known as phytoplankton and minute animals known as zooplankton, that drift near the surface of the water. It is eaten by many sea creatures including baleen whales. They have huge comb-like sieves hanging down from the roofs of their mouths which trap the plankton.

Q What is the biggest creature in the sea?

A The blue whale weighs 168 tons, and can measure 108 ft. long. It is harmless though, feeding only on tiny zooplankton called krill. It needs to sieve 4.5 tons of krill a day to survive!

Q How many species of fish are there?

A So far more than 21,000 species of fish have been recorded. The largest fish is the whale shark, measuring 59 ft. long. The smallest fish is the dwarf goby, measuring less than $\frac{1}{4}$ in. long - it will fit on the end of a human fingernail!

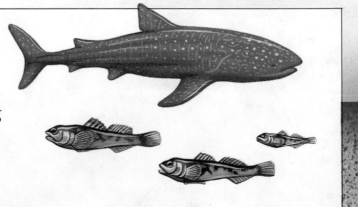

Dolphins are very friendly creatures. They often swim alongside ships for miles, leaping out of the water.

Whales sing to each other underwater. Their eerie wails can be heard miles away.

Q What mammals live in the sea?

A Seals, whales and dolphins are all sea mammals. Like mammals on land they are warm-blooded, have a backbone and hair, breathe air and take care of their young after they are born.

Q What creatures live on the seabed?

A The open, sandy seabed offers few places to hide. Most of the creatures that live there have flat bodies and are well camouflaged so they can lie hidden from predators and prey. Rays, plaice and other flatfish live on the seabed.

Q What is the most feared animal in the sea?

A Humans have a fear of sharks, especially the great white shark. However, many sharks are harmless. The great white is unlikely to attack a human unless provoked or if it mistakes a swimmer for a seal or turtle on which it normally feeds.

Q Do any creatures live in the ocean depths?

A Some weird and wonderful creatures have been discovered living in the darkest depths of the ocean. Many of them are extremely scary with little eyes, huge mouths and fang-like teeth. Viper fish, gulper eels and the deep sea angler fish all look like they are from a horror film!

In 1969 four scientists lived in a special home, called Tektite, on the seabed for sixty days!

What is in the ocean depths?

Humans have only been able to explore the depths of the oceans in the last century. Expensive, highly technical equipment is needed for us to breathe and cope with the extreme cold and pressure.

Q How do we explore the ocean depths?

A We need underwater crafts like submersibles, submarines and bathyscaphes. These are all specially designed to protect the crew from high pressure underwater and enables them to work for fairly long periods without returning to the surface. Small submersibles can travel down to 3,900 ft. and stay there for 48 hours, while a large nuclear submarine can stay submerged for months!

Q How do we know how deep the sea is?

A We can measure the depth of the sea with an echo sounder. Sound waves are bounced off the seabed back to an echo sounder in a boat. Scientists can work out the depth from how long it takes for the sound waves to travel back.

Q How deep has a submersible traveled beneath the sea?

A On January 23, 1960, a bathyscaphe called *Trieste* reached the bottom of the Marianas Trench, the deepest part of the ocean. It took them 4 hours and 48 minutes to travel 36,202 ft.

Trieste

A diver coming up too quickly from the deep can get "the bends." Nitrogen gas gets trapped in the joints causing extreme pain.

Deep sea angler fish have a glowing light dangling in front of their mouths to attract prey.

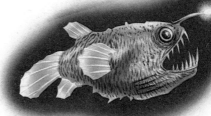

Q Is there light in the ocean depths?

A No. No light at all penetrates deeper than 3,200 ft. Most light filters out at 32 ft. Not only does the sea get darker the deeper you go, but it also gets colder. At 13,000 ft. deep it is as cold as the inside of a refridgerator.

Q How do deep sea creatures see?

A Some creatures which live in the dark ocean depths produce their own light called bioluminescence. This light helps them to see where they are going, trap prey and find a mate in the dark. Flashlight fish have two light organs under each eye, made up of billions of microscopic glowing bacteria.

Q Are there seaquakes?

A Yes. Many seaquakes happen in the "Ring of Fire" around the Pacific Ocean. Most are never felt above or even near the surface.

Q Are there underwater mountains?

A Yes. Some mountains underwater are so huge their peaks rise out above the surface. The highest mountain on Earth is not Mount Everest, but Mount Kea in the Pacific Ocean. It is a volcanic mountain which rises a staggering 33,476 ft. off the sea floor.

Q What is on the ocean floor?

A When a marine animal or plant dies it is either eaten or its body drifts down to the seabed to decay. About 75 percent of the deep ocean floor is covered in a thick ooze made up from the decaying bodies of plants and animals and mud. In most places this ooze is 1,900 ft. thick, but in some places it can be up to 6 miles thick!

Thousands of tiny islands in the Pacific Ocean are made entirely of coral.

What is a coral reef?

Coral reefs are as important in the sea as rainforests are on the land. They provide shelter and feeding grounds for fish and other sea creatures and protect coastlines. As a major tourist attraction coral reefs also provide a large income for some countries.

Q How is a coral reef made?

A Coral reefs are built by millions of tiny animals called polyps. Each animal grows a tough, chalky outer skeleton to protect its soft body. When polyps die, these tough outer cases build up on top of one another over the centuries forming the framework of massive coral reefs.

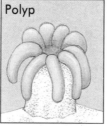
Polyp

Q What lives in a coral reef?

A The rich food supply carried in the water surrounding coral reefs, plus the shelter they offer, attracts hundreds of colorful and exotic sea creatures. Parrot fish, angel fish, butterfly fish and lion fish can be seen swimming around. Anemones, starfish, sea slugs and clams cling to the coral.

Q What are some of the weirdest creatures living in coral reefs?

A Puffer fish blow themselves up like balloons to defend themselves. Some fish, like sea dragons, have flaps of skin to disguise themselves among rocks and seaweed.

Puffer fish

Trigger fish

Sea dragon

Angel fish

The Great Barrier Reef has taken at least 15 million years to get to its present size.

The parrot fish makes a special jelly-like bubble around itself for protection at night.

Q Where are coral reefs found?

A Big, colorful coral reefs are found only in tropical and semi-tropical seas, such as the Red Sea. However, some small, non-reef-building corals can be found in colder waters, like cup corals. Coral reefs grow best at 23-65 ft. below the surface of the sea, in clean water at 68-79°F.

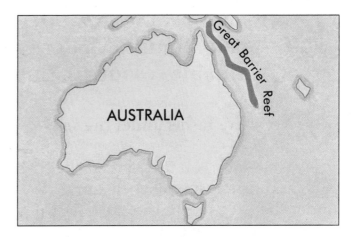

AUSTRALIA

Great Barrier Reef

Q What destroys coral reefs?

A Some creatures actually eat the coral. Parrot fish break off lumps of coral with their sharp beaks, while the crown of thorns starfish can eat 46-62 sq. in. of coral in one day! The reefs are also being destroyed by people.

Q Which is the largest coral reef?

A The Great Barrier Reef off the coast of Queensland in Australia is the largest coral reef in the world. It stretches for 1,260 mi. and covers an area of 79,923 sq. mi. The reef is so huge it can even be seen from the Moon!

Q Which coral reef creatures can be dangerous?

A Most sea creatures are not dangerous unless frightened. Six-foot moray eels lurk under rocks, waiting to lunge out at their prey. Sting rays have poisonous spines on the end of their long, whip-like tails. People have died after standing on the highly poisonous stone fish which looks like the rough surface of coral.

Lion fish

Sting ray

Stone fish

Icebergs are made of fresh water. They could be towed to countries suffering from drought and melted for drinking water.

How do we use the sea?

Ever since people inhabited the Earth, we have relied on it for many things. Modern technology means we can extract valuable resources, important to modern living.

Q Are there farms under the sea?

A Yes. Many countries breed shellfish and fish in special enclosures under the sea as it is easier to collect them and they can control the conditions to make them grow faster and bigger. The Japanese have underwater seaweed farms as they like to eat it. Salt farms trap and dry the salt in seawater and it is then cleaned.

Salt farm

Seaweed drying

Oyster farm

Lobster

Q Why are whales killed?

A Today only a few countries kill whales, and the numbers they are allowed to kill is restricted. However, the way in which they are killed is cruel and organizations like Greenpeace are trying to stop whaling completely. Many products contain whale including oil, pet foods, cosmetics, candles and fertilizers.

Q How is energy made from the waves?

A The tumbling motion of the waves is used to make electricity. Special giant rockers which float on the surface of the water are pushed up and down by the force of the waves. This pushes water through a shaft inside, which in turn drives a turbine, and so makes a constant source of electricity.

A large oil rig may produce enough oil in one day to fill 70,000 cars with gasoline!

Six million tons of salt are taken from the sea each year for commercial use.

Q What sea creatures do we eat?

A Each year over 70 million tons of fish are caught in the oceans for food. Cockles, mussels, oysters, lobsters and crabs provide us with seafood.

Q How is energy made from the tides?

A Tidal power stations channel water through tunnels and past large blades. The force of the water coming in and going out turns the blades, which drive turbines, spinning a generator which produces electricity.

Q Can you drink seawater?

A You should avoid drinking seawater because the salt and chemicals in it will make you sick. However, it can be drunk if the water is boiled and distilled and the salt evaporated.

Q How is oil extracted from the seabed?

A Once oil is found, it is extracted by drilling deep down into the seabed to make an oil well from which oil can be pumped. The oil is then transported away from the oil rig, either by pipelines to the shore, or if the rig is right out at sea, by huge oil tankers which can carry 550,000 tons of oil in one trip!

Q What other valuable resources come from the sea?

A Sand and gravel are extracted in huge amounts for commercial use. Shells and sponges are collected and sold. Diamonds are sucked up from the seabed off Southwest Africa. Pearls are collected from oysters. Gold has even been mined off the coasts of Alaska.

Sand Gravel Pearls Shells Diamonds Gold

The furthest a sailboat has ever sailed in a day is 462 miles.

How do we enjoy the sea?

For centuries, people all over the world have found pleasure in the sea, using it to swim, dive or fish in, sail or surf on, either for competitive sport or just for fun.

Q Who swam the longest ocean swim?

A The longest ocean swim was undertaken by Walter Poenisch in the Atlantic Ocean. In July, 1978, he swam from Cuba to Florida in 34 hours, 15 minutes!

Florida

Cuba

Q What is the record for swimming the English Channel?

A In 1978 Penny Dean swam the English Channel in 7 hours, 40 minutes from Dover in England to Cap Gris-Nez in France.

Q What is the quickest time for sailing around the world?

A It took Frenchman Bruno Peyron and his crew just 79 days, 6 hours, 16 minutes to sail nonstop around world. They completed this massive journey on April 20, 1993.

Q How deep is the deepest underwater dive?

A The record for an underwater breath-held dive stands at 350 ft., achieved by Angela Bandini on October 3, 1989. She was underwater for 2 minutes, 36 seconds! However, with the aid of SCUBA diving equipment, a dive of 436 ft. has been made. In 1992 Theo Mavrostomos dived to a staggering 2,300 ft. using SCUBA equipment filled with a special mixture of oxygen, helium and hydrogen.

Channel swimmers cover themselves in thick grease to protect them against the cold water.

A record 100 water skiers were towed together for over a mile off the coast of Australia in 1986.

Q Who were the first people to sail?

A The Ancient Egyptians were the first people known to sail 5,000 years ago. Their sails were square and made out of reeds. Today some of the biggest sailing boats have as many as 30 sails and need about 200 people to raise and lower them.

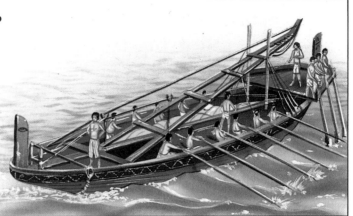

Q What is the highest wave surfed?

A The highest wave ever ridden was a tidal wave that struck Hawaii on April 3, 1868. To save his life, a Hawaiian named Holua rode this massive 540 ft. wave. Good surfers regularly ride waves between 30-36 ft. high off Waimea Bay in Hawaii.

Q How fast is the fastest waterskier?

A The fastest record for waterskiing is held by Christopher Massey. On March 6, 1983, he traveled at 143 mph.

Even today, some people pay homage to the sea god Neptune when they cross the Equator for the first time.

What sea legends are there?

In the 15th Century people believed that the Earth was flat and that if you sailed too far from land you would fall off the edge!

Many unexplained mysteries surround the sea. Sailors returning from long jouneys often told stories of huge sea monsters and mermaids.

Q Do mermaids really exist?

A Nobody really knows if mermaids exist, but it is unlikely. The manatee, a plant-eating marine mammal, may be the source of this famous legend. The female manatee floats upright while nursing her young, using her front feet to cradle it. From a distance, this might look like a human mother with her baby in her arms.

Q Where is the lost island of Atlantis supposed to be?
A Legend has it that the beautiful island of Atlantis sunk without a trace with all its inhabitants after a massive volcanic eruption. It has never been found, but some believe it is under the sea near the Greek or Canary Islands.

Q What was the *Marie Celeste*?

A The *Marie Celeste* was a large ship which was found on December 3, 1872 drifting in the Atlantic Ocean. Mysteriously, all of the crew had completely vanished, leaving their breakfasts half-eaten on the table! To this day no clues to the crew's whereabouts have been found.

Q What is the Bermuda Triangle?

A The Bermuda Triangle is a large area of the Atlantic Ocean that stretches between Bermuda, Puerto Rico and Florida where ships and aircraft have mysteriously disappeared without a trace. Some people believe that they have been kidnapped by UFOs!

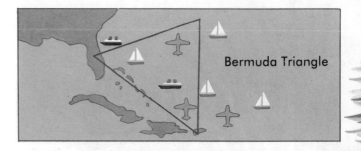

Bermuda Triangle

The giant squid has the biggest eyes of any animal. They are 17 times bigger than human eyes, measuring 16 in. across.

Q Are there really sea monsters?

A There are many stories of krakens, huge octopus-like creatures, which could easily turn over a ship. This legend is probably based on the giant squid. Although they do not grow big enough to over turn a large ship, they can weigh up to two tons and measure 50 ft. long!

Neptune

Q Who are the ocean gods?

A For thousands of years, many cultures across the world have worshipped sea gods and goddesses, hoping they will keep them safe on long journeys across the sea or bring them luck when fishing.

Q What is the *Flying Dutchman*?

A The *Flying Dutchman* is a famous ghost ship. The story has it that the ship left Amsterdam in the seventeenth century for the East Indies and ran into a fierce storm. Her captain, dared by a ghostly devil, sailed right into the storm, wrecking his ship and killing everyone aboard. The ship and her crew continue to haunt the seas, bringing bad luck to all that see her.

An estimated 2 million sea birds and 10,000 marine mammals are killed each year due to human waste dumped into the sea.

How do we care for the sea?

The sea, like the land, is suffering badly from pollution. For many years the sea has been used as a dumping ground for a variety of human waste products, all of which can have harmful effects on the creatures that live there.

Q What are the main causes of sea pollution?

A There are five main causes of pollution to the sea:
1) Nuclear waste from power stations.
2) Trash and heavy metals from industry, like lead and mercury.
3) Chemicals washed from the land into rivers and the sea, like fertilizers and pesticides.
4) Oil from coastal industries, ships and tanker spillages.
5) Sewage pumped into the sea.

Q Why is Minamata Bay in Japan famous?

A Between 1953 and 1960 hundreds of villagers in Minamata Bay in Japan were poisoned and 649 people died. This is because they had eaten shellfish contaminated with mercury which had been dumped into the sea by local industries.

Q What is being done about pollution?

A Recently environmental groups like Greenpeace and some governments are promoting a new theory called "clean production." This means that scientists are designing production processes and products that have no, or very little, toxic waste and so will cause minimum damage to the environment.

Q What is sewage?

A Sewage is waste which comes from homes, offices, shops and factories. It is 99 percent water but also contains lots of harmful chemicals like ammonia. The sewage is separated into solids and liquids and then pumped into the sea, causing terrible pollution in some areas.

Over 1 billion gallons of sewage is dumped into our coastal waters every day, most of which is untreated.

50 percent of the household trash thrown away is packaging, costing 633 million dollars a year.

Q What can you do to help?

A You should think about waste and how to recycle it. Here are some things you can do:
1) Try not to buy goods with lots of wrapping.
2) Find out if and where local recycling stations for paper, cans, bottles and clothes are.
3) Cut down on electricity by turning off lights when you are not in a room.
4) Try walking or cycling short distances with your family instead of taking the car.

Q What sea creatures are in danger?

A Some sea creatures have already become extinct. Many more are in danger, such as those pictured in the panel opposite.

Q When was one of the largest oil tanker accidents?

A In March, 1989 the massive oil tanker, the *Exxon Valdez*, ran aground in Alaska where it poured 12 million gallons of oil into the sea. This killed an estimated 100,000 sea birds and hundreds of thousands of fish, seals and shellfish.

Blue whale

Fin whale

Mediterranean monk seal

Kemp's ridley turtle

Sea otter

Florida manatee

Forty years ago floods
killed 1,400 people in
the Netherlands, and
307 in England.

What is the sea's future?

Temperatures around the world are gradually rising, known as global warming. This is having severe effects on the environment, including the sea.

Q What is the "Greenhouse Effect?"

A The "Greenhouse Effect" is the term used to describe how the Earth is kept warm by gases in the atmosphere trapping heat. Scientists believe that the "Greenhouse Effect" is increasing as more of the gases are being given off into the atmosphere.

Q Which gases are harmful?

A Carbon dioxide and water vapor are the main greenhouse gases. Carbon dioxide is given off by power stations and factories. It is also given off as forests are burned to make way for farmland and building. Chlorofluorocarbons (CFCs) are given off by aerosol sprays and refrigerators. Nitrous oxides come from car exhaust fumes and from fertilizers. Methane is given off from rotting vegetation and trash.

Q What is an El Nino?

A An El Nino is a large, natural current which occurs about every five years in the Pacific Ocean. This current causes the sea level to fall, the water temperature to rise, torrential rain to fall and coral reefs to die. This is only a temporary disaster which gives us an example of what could happen worldwide if global warming continues.

When unusually warm waters entered the Galapagos coral reefs in 1983, more than 90 percent of the coral died.

The sea temperature only has to increase by 5 or 6°F and all the coral will die!

Q What is coral bleaching?

A Coral is the first to show signs of suffering when the sea temperature rises. It causes them to go completely white (to bleach!). Tiny plants called Zooxanthellae live inside them, providing their food and giving them their color. As soon as the water gets warmer these tiny plants are expelled from the coral. At first the coral loses its color, but eventually it will die.

Q Is the sea level rising?

A Many scientists believe that as temperatures are increasing (called global warming), the sea level is rising at an average rate of 1/4 to 1/2 in. per year. They think this is due to mountain glaciers melting.

Q What happens as the sea level rises?

A Rising water levels cause flooding, and this in turn causes erosion of the land. This can have disastrous consequences as more than 70 percent of the world's population live on the coasts.

Q What will happen in the future?

A It is predicted that the sea level will rise by 1 to 4 in. each year in the future, if the temperature continues to increase at the present rate. Changes in the climate could mean an increase in violent storms with tsunamis and hurricanes causing coastal damage. Coastal cities under threat include Alexandria, Venice, Shanghai and London. Whole islands could disappear.

Planet Mars also spins with a tilted axis so it has seasons very similar to Earth.

Mars

What is weather?

People who study the weather are called meteorologists. People who study climate are called climatologists.

Weather is the name given to the changing conditions of the atmosphere, or air, which surrounds the Earth. Weather conditions include wind, storms, rain, snow and sunshine.

Q What is climate?

A The average weather conditions over a long period of time - usually 10 to 30 years.

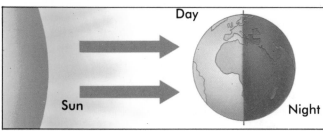

Day

Sun

Night

Q Why do we have day and night?

A Once every 24 hours the Earth spins around on its axis (an imaginary line joining the North Pole, the center of the Earth and the South Pole), turning us toward the light of the Sun and away again, thus giving us night and day.

Q What is atmosphere?

A The mixture of gases which surround the Earth, made up of nitrogen, oxygen, water vapor and tiny amounts of other gases. Without these protective gases, human beings could not survive on Earth. They protect us from the scorching rays of the Sun and from the icy chill of the night.

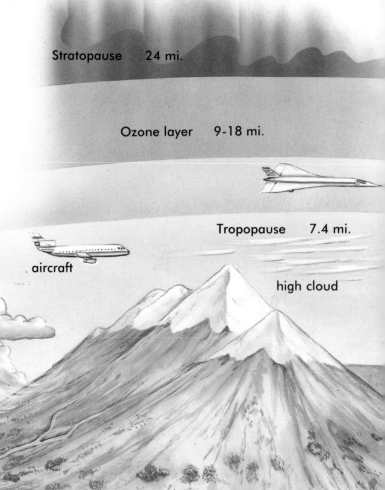

Stratopause   24 mi.

Ozone layer   9-18 mi.

Tropopause   7.4 mi.

aircraft

high cloud

A meteorologist

The hottest place on Earth is Dallol in Ethiopia, where the average temperature is 94°F in the shade.

Q How is the atmosphere held around the Earth?

A The force of gravity pulls the gases of the atmosphere toward the Earth and prevents them from escaping into space.

Q Which are the hottest and coldest times of the day?

A The hottest time of the day is usually around 2 or 3 pm, while the coldest time is usually at sunrise.

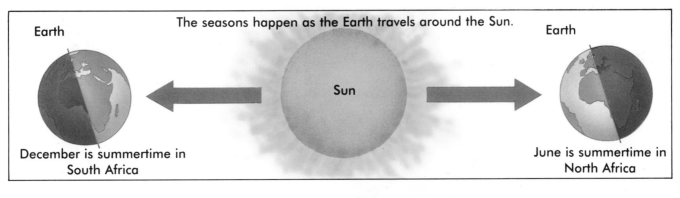

The seasons happen as the Earth travels around the Sun.

Earth

Sun

Earth

December is summertime in South Africa

June is summertime in North Africa

Q Why do we have seasons?

A The four seasons - spring, summer, autumn and winter - are caused by the tilt of the Earth's axis. As the Earth moves around on its axis different parts are tilted toward the Sun for a few months at a time. The part leaning towards the Sun has summer, while the part leaning away has winter.

The weather happens in the lowest level of the atmosphere.

Q Where are the hottest and coldest places on Earth?

A The tropical regions, close to the Equator, are the hottest because the Sun's rays are most concentrated there. The coldest places are the North Pole and the South Pole, where the Sun is so low in the sky that its power is spread over a vast area.

North Pole

Equator

South Pole

135

What is air pressure?

Although we cannot see it, air has weight which causes it to press down on the Earth and everything on it. Changes in the air pressure affect the weather.

Q Why is air pressure important to weather forecasters?

A Air pressure changes constantly, bringing different types of weather. These changes help weather forecasters to predict rainy weather, which usually comes with low pressure, and dry weather, which comes with high pressure.

Q Can we feel air pressure?

A No, not usually. However, occasionally when you go up or down a hill in a car, your ears may feel funny due to the change of air pressure. The same thing can happen in an aircraft.

Mt. Everest - 320 millibars

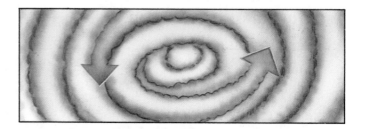

Q How do meteorologists measure the changes in air pressure?

A Pressure is measured with a barometer in units called millibars. Aneroid barometers contain hollow capsules with no air inside. As the pressure of the air alters, the capsules change shape and slowly move the pointer on the dial to show whether the air pressure is rising or falling.

An aneroid barometer

Q Why is air pressure lower at the top of mountains?

A Because there is less air pressing down from above. The lower air pressure makes the air thinner and harder to breathe.

High ground - 900 millibars

The cabins of aircraft are specially pressurized so that the crew and passengers it carries do not suffer from the difference in air pressure the higher the plane flies.

If you carry a barometer in an elevator you will see the air pressure drop as you travel upward.

Q What is Buys Ballot's Law?

A It is the law for wind direction which states that when you stand with your back to the wind in the northern hemisphere you have high pressure on your right and low pressure on your left. In the southern hemisphere it is the reverse.

Low pressure

Q What is an isobar?

A Isobars are lines on weather maps that link places with the same air pressure. Weather people use these maps to forecast the weather for the next day.

Isobars are usually shown at intervals of 4 millibars.

The further apart isobars are, the lighter the wind.

Q What is the normal pressure on low ground, near sea level?

A Normal pressure at this low level is about 1,000 millibars.

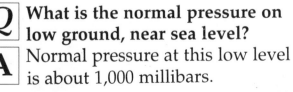

Sea level - 1,000 millibars

What is wind?

A weather vane shows the wind direction.

Wind is air moving from one place to another as it warms up or cools down.

Q What makes the wind blow?

A The wind blows because cold air is continually moving in to replace rising warm air. As the Sun warms up different parts of the Earth's surface, the air above it is also warmed. Warm air becomes lighter and rises above surrounding cold air. In other places, the air cools, becomes heavier and sinks.

cold air sinks

warm air rises

cold air moves in

Q How is wind speed measured?

A An instrument called an anemometer measures wind speed. It has three or four metal cups at the end of arms which blow around slowly in a light breeze. The faster the wind blows, the faster the cups spin round.

An anemometer

Q What is the Beaufort Scale?

A This is a method of estimating the wind speed if you don't have an anemometer.

Force 1 - smoke drifts slowly

Force 2 - leaves rustle

Force 3 - leaves and small twigs move

Force 4 - small branches move

Force 5 - small trees with leaves sway

Force 6 - large branches move

Force 7 - whole trees sway

Gale force 8 - twigs break off trees, and walking is difficult

Jet Streams are very strong winds high up in the atmosphere - at about the same height as jet aircraft fly. They can reach 186 mph or more.

Q What is a tornado?

A This is a small whirling spiral of strong wind. Although much smaller than a hurricane, it is very powerful and can toss people, cars and even buildings into the air. There is more about tornadoes on page 150.

Powerful tornadoes are common in the central U.S., especially in the area known as "tornado alley" through Kansas and Oklahoma.

Q What is a hurricane?

A They are violent storms that start when warm, wet air over the sea rises and forms huge columns of cloud full of water vapor. More air rushes in below the rising warm air and begins to spiral around at up to 186 mph. These fierce winds cause massive waves at sea and sometimes on the coast. When they hit the land they often cause enormous destruction.

A typical Mediterranean windmill

Q What is the difference between a gust of wind and a lull?

A A gust is an abrupt rush of wind. A lull is when the wind gets lighter for a few seconds.

Q How can people use the wind?

A Wind power can be used in various ways. In flat countries people still use windmills to grind corn and pump water. Some countries, such as Britain, build wind generators to generate electricity. The wind can also be used for windsurfing, sailing and for flying kites.

A modern wind generator

When air is forced upward over a barrier such as hills or mountains, clouds form.

What are clouds?

Clouds are made up of billions of tiny drops of water. They form in different shapes and at different heights in the sky.

Q How does a cloud form?

A A cloud forms when moist air rises upward. As the air cools, it expands and changes, or condenses, into tiny water droplets. The highest clouds contain ice crystals.

Warm air rises   It condenses   A cloud forms

Q Can aircraft fly through clouds?

A Yes, very easily. The water drops, or ice crystals, are so tiny that they barely affect an aircraft's progress. Usually an aircraft will climb through the clouds into the sunshine above.

Q Why do scientists study clouds?

A Scientists in weather stations around the world make daily observations of cloud formations. The results help them forecast the kind of weather to come.

Aircraft sometimes leave artificial cloud trails behind them, called contrails. They are made of ice crystals.

Q What are the highest clouds?

A There are three types of high clouds: *cirrus* clouds form in thin wispy streaks; *cirrostratus* clouds make a pale, high layer; and *cirrocumulus* are tiny lumps of cloud that look like beads or pearls.

Cirrus

Cirrostratus

Cirrocumulus

Altocumulus

Q What clouds form the middle cloud layer

A There are three types: *altocumulus* clouds that form a higher, lumpy layer; *altostratus* clouds, making a pale, white layer; and *nimbostratus* clouds - a gray layer which produces rain or snow.

Nimbostratus

Altostratus

Cumulonimbus

Q What are the lowest clouds?

A There are four types of low clouds. *Stratus* clouds form a low, gray layer that often covers the tops of hills; *stratocumulus* clouds make an uneven patchy layer; *cumulus* clouds - sometimes called "cotton-wool" clouds; and *cumulonimbus* clouds, the dark, storm clouds.

Cumulus

Stratocumulus

Stratus

The driest place in the world is the Atacama desert in Chile, where the rainfall is less than 0.004 in. per year.

Rain provides the water that is necessary for the survival of plants, animals and humans. Without rain almost the only life on Earth would be in the oceans.

Q What makes it rain?

A As the Sun heats up Earth's oceans and rivers, water turns into an invisible gas called water vapor. As the vapor rises it turns into water droplets, which eventually form a cloud. The droplets continue growing until they are so heavy that they fall to the ground as rain. In this way, the same water evaporates and turns into rain again and again. This is known as the water cycle.

3. Water vapor turns into water droplets that form into clouds.

2. Water turns into water vapor and rises.

4. Water droplets grow and fall as rain.

1. Water is heated by the Sun's rays.

The cycle begins again.

Q What is humidity?

A Humidity is the amount of moisture in the air. Very humid air can be a sign of wet weather to come.

Q How is rainfall measured?

A Each day, rain collects in a rain gauge. This is often a simple metal container which catches the rain in a funnel at the top.

Q Does the amount of rainfall have much affect on the environment

A Yes. In areas where the rainfall is heavy, such as the rain forests around the Equator, there are many different kinds of plants and animals. However, in deserts - where the rainfall is less than 10 in. per year - there is very little plant or animal life.

Many deserts have no rain for years.

In rainforests, it rains nearly every day.

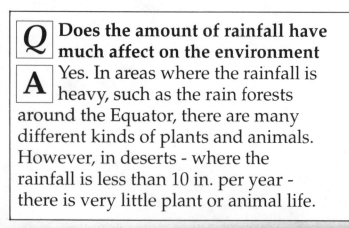

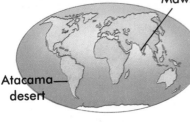

Mawsynram

Atacama desert

The wettest place in the world is thought to be Mawsynran in India, with 475 in. of rain per year. However, there may be wetter places where the rainfall has not been measured.

143

Q What causes floods?

A In hot countries floods are usually caused by thunderstorms. In cooler climates, low pressure areas may bring rain several times in a week until the rivers overflow their banks. Sometimes melting snow causes floods.

Severe drought makes soil dry out and crops fail. This can lead to the death of animals and people.

Q What is a monsoon?

A Monsoons bring heavy rains to India, Bangladesh and other parts of Asia every summer. The word "monsoon" actually means a steady wind. However, because these summer-time winds bring heavy rains, monsoon is often used to describe the rains rather than the wind. In India the torrential rains which the monsoon brings - known as the rainy season - are vital to farmers because most of the annual rainfall falls during them.

Q What is a drought?

A A drought is when a lack of rain over a long period causes a water shortage. For many years the Sahel region of Africa suffered an almost continual drought. The people there were unable to grow crops or feed their animals, and thousands of people and animals died.

Monsoon rains often lead to flooding.

Some animals, such as Polar bears, are specially adapted to live in a snowy climate.

When does it snow?

The heaviest snowfalls tend to occur when the temperature is around freezing point.

Q What makes it snow?

A When it is very cold the water in clouds freezes and forms snow crystals. As these crystals fall through the clouds they join with others and become snowflakes.

Q When is snow a nuisance or a danger?

A In heavy winds, snow can be blown into huge piles called snowdrifts. Snowdrifts block roads, and have to be cleared by big tractors with snowploughs on the front. In rural areas, snowdrifts can cut off whole villages, and supplies have to be dropped by helicopters. Snow can also bring down power lines, cutting off people's electricity.

Q When does the coldest weather occur?

A In most countries the coldest times are clear, calm nights when there are no clouds to keep the heat near the Earth's surface.

Q Can snow be useful?

A Yes. It can help crops - such as winter wheat - by protecting them from very hard frosts and cold dry winds. Also, it can be fun for skiing, sledding and for making snowballs and snowmen. In the past, the Inuit people of northern Canada and Greenland built houses, called igloos, out of snow.

Hailstones can weigh more than a pound. In 1986 a hailstorm in Bangladesh killed 92 people.

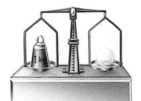

All snowflakes have six sides, but no two are ever the same.

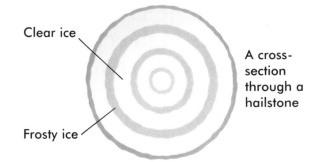

Clear ice

Frosty ice

A cross-section through a hailstone

Hailstones are frozen raindrops that form in cumulonimbus clouds. As they fall through the cloud they melt, then freeze, making frosty and icy layers.

Q Can it snow during a thunderstorm?

A Yes, but this is quite rare. It might happen during the winter, particularly on the coast.

Q What is a blizzard?

A A blizzard is a snowstorm. Loose, powdery snow is whipped up by strong winds, sometimes making it impossible to see anything.

Q What is the difference between snow and hail?

A Snowflakes are much lighter than hailstones, and have more air trapped inside. Hailstones are hard and heavy, like icy pellets. Hail comes out of cumulonimbus clouds, and can even fall in summer.

In very cold weather beautiful frost patterns sometimes form on windows. Some people call this fern-like pattern "Jack Frost's Garden."

Q What is a frost?

A A frost is a temperature below freezing point. During a frost, ice crystals form on the grass or on the ground. Sometimes it looks so white that it could be mistaken for snow.

Benjamin Franklin's experiment with a kite linked to a metal key showed what lightning was made of, when the key gave off sparks of electricity.

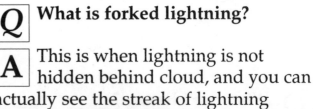

What causes thunderstorms?

When humid air rises quickly, cumulonimbus clouds form. Scientists think that ice crystals in the clouds rub together, creating electricity which is released as a flash of lightning. The lightning heats the air, causing it to expand rapidly and creating the noise of thunder.

Q Can you get thunder without lightning?

A No, the two things always go together. Sometimes you might hear the thunder when you have missed seeing the lighting. At night you may see lightning but be too far away to hear the thunder.

Q What should you do if you are caught in a thunderstorm?

A Lightning tends to strike high things, such as tall trees and buildings, so if you are caught in a thunderstorm out in the open, crouch down on the ground or run for the shelter of a car or building. Do not take shelter under trees - this could be very dangerous!

Q What is sheet lightning?

A This is when the lightning is hidden by cloud but you can still see the brightness of the flash.

Q What is forked lightning?

A This is when lightning is not hidden behind cloud, and you can actually see the streak of lightning between cloud and ground. The streak is sometimes split into two or three branches. There is actually no difference between sheet and fork lightning other than the way you see it.

The places with most thunderstorms a year are near the Equator. Bogor in Java has more than 220 thunderstorms. The least thundery places are in the Arctic and Antarctic.

Arctic

Java

Antarctic

Lightning takes the quickest route to the ground, so it usually hits high buildings or trees. Most high buildings are fitted with a lightning conductor that carries the electric charge safely to the ground.

Q How can you measure the distance of a thunderstorm?

A When you see lightning, start counting the seconds until you hear the thunder. Divide the number of seconds by five to get the distance away in miles. To get the distance in kilometers, divide the number of seconds by three. This delay between thunder and lightning occurs because light travels much faster than sound.

Q What is St. Elmo's Fire?

A This is static electricity which sometimes makes the masts of ships glow with light during thunderstorms.

Q Do tornadoes and thunderstorms ever occur together?

A Yes, sometimes. They both come with cumulonimbus clouds, though a tornado will only form with a very powerful cumulonimbus.

Q Can people be struck by lightning and survive?

A Yes. An American, Roy Sullivan, has been struck by lightning seven times and survived. However, occasionally cattle, sheep and even people are killed.

A severe gale at sea can create waves more than 50 ft. high.

Is weather different at sea?

The most important difference between sea and land is the temperature. It is normally cooler at sea than inland during the day, but warmer at night.

Q Is the wind stronger over the sea?

A Yes, because the open sea has no hills, trees or buildings to slow down its speed.

Q What is a sea breeze?

A This is a wind that blows from the sea on to the coast on a warm, sunny day. It happens because the air over the land is heated up more quickly than the air over the sea. The warm air over the land rises and a current of cooler air moves in from the sea to replace it.

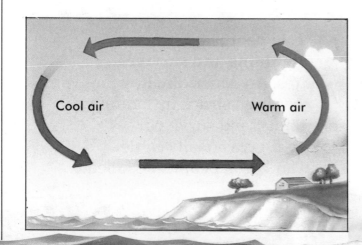

Cool air

Warm air

Q Is humidity different near the sea?

A Humidity is higher near the sea because water evaporates into the air. Evaporation is when water is warmed up and turned into water vapor. This is why puddles dry up on a sunny day.

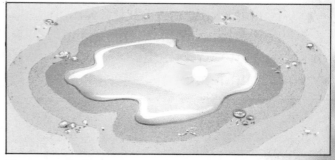

On a sunny day, water evaporates, or dries up.

Q Do you get fog or thunder at sea?

A Yes, these can both occur. Fog is quite common in areas of cold sea, while thunder is common in hot regions, such as the Caribbean and Central Pacific.

At sea, gales, fogs and storms can make conditions dangerous for sailors.

Waves can arrive on the beach even when the weather is calm. These waves are caused by gales or strong winds which have occurred perhaps 1,800 mi. away.

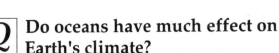

Grand Banks, near Newfoundland, Canada, is the world's foggiest area of sea.

Q Is the weather better in coastal places than inland?

A It varies! Areas around the coast tend to be wetter and foggier than inland. Sea breezes mean that summers are also generally cooler. However, there is much less frost in coastal areas and winters are normally milder.

Q Do oceans have much effect on Earth's climate?

A Yes, they absorb the Sun's heat and spread it around the world in currents. These currents are huge wind-driven rivers in the sea that heat or cool the air above them, creating hotter or cooler weather.

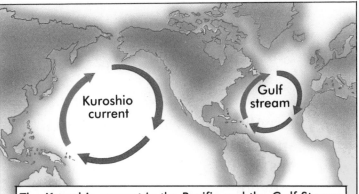

The Kuroshio current in the Pacific and the Gulf Stream in the Atlantic carry warm water northward.

Q What weather conditions can be dangerous to sailors?

A Fog can drastically reduce visibility at sea. However, lighthouses, sirens, foghorns and radar all help ships to find their way in dense fogs. Gales can be more of a problem, whipping up waves and causing ships to slow down or even capsize.

In Canada's Rocky Mountains, warm winds blow that can raise the temperature by 50°F.

All parts of the world occasionally get bizarre weather conditions. There have even been reports of red rain and summer snow.

Q Are there any cases of unusual snowfall?

A Yes. In 1975, snow in England prevented a summer cricket match, while in September, 1981, snow fell in the Kalahari Desert, Africa, for the first time in living memory.

Q What causes colored snow and rain to fall on the Alps?

A Red, pink and brown rain or snow sometimes falls over the Alps. This is caused by the colored dust of the Sahara Desert being swept over 1,242 mi. by the wind.

Q What is a waterspout?

A A waterspout is simply a tornado that forms over the sea. It is a swirling column of air that sucks up seawater and other things in its path. Although waterspouts are not as powerful as the tornadoes that form over land, they can still be very dangerous, especially to small boats. In the past, sailors used to think that distant waterspouts were sea monsters rising up from the waves!

Q Do unidentifiable substances ever fall from the sky?

A Yes, over the years there have been numerous reports of slimy material falling out of the sky. In 1978, a green slime fell on Washington, coating cars and buildings, killing plants and making animals sick. It has been suggested that the slime was caused by pesticide and jet exhaust fumes, but this has not been proven. Some people believe that these slimy materials could come from some sort of alien life form!

Sometimes it can be raining on one side of a house while the Sun is shining on the other side. This usually happens when the edge of a cumulonimbus cloud is overhead.

Q What is El Nino?

A This is a sudden warming every few years of the Pacific Ocean off the coast of South America. It spreads westward and affects the weather of many countries. It is not yet fully understood.

Waterspouts are tornadoes that happen at sea.

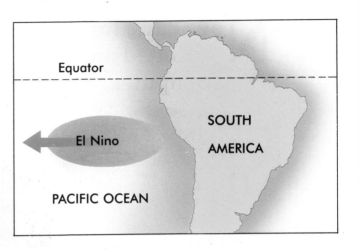

Equator

El Nino

SOUTH AMERICA

PACIFIC OCEAN

Q What is the world's record rainburst?

A In 1970, 1.5 in. of rain fell on Guadeloupe, in the West Indies, in just 90 seconds.

Q Can it really rain "cats and dogs?"

A There don't appear to be any reports of it actually raining cats and dogs. However, there are reliable records from around the world of showers of fish, frogs, spiders, crabs and other creatures. Apparently, on June 16, 1939 a shower of tiny frogs fell on Trowbridge in England. It would seem that strong winds and waterspouts can suck up a whole variety of things and drop them some distance away.

How are forecasts made?

Nowadays, information from around the world is plotted on a synoptic chart and then fed into a computer. The computer works out what the next day's weather might be.

Q How is weather information collected?

A There are over 10,000 weather stations around the world. Many are in major cities and airports, while others are on weather ships. People working there make regular checks on visibility, wind speed and direction, humidity, air pressure and rainfall. In other places balloons are launched to collect upper air information about jet streams and cold air above. Satellites also circle the Earth, sending down cloud and temperature patterns. Radar picks up signs of coming rain and storms.

Weather balloon

Radar

Weather ship

Q Is it easier to make very short range forecasts?

A Yes. A radar display will show us where it is raining now, and can compute where the rain will be in the next two hours.

Radar weather picture

Q How accurate are weather forecasts?

A Although weather forecasts try to be as accurate as possible, they are not always correct. Weather forecasters claim to be right eight out of ten times.

The word "forecast" was first used to describe weather prediction in 1850 by Britain's then Chief Meteorologist, Admiral Fitzroy.

Some early meteorologists named hurricanes after people they didn't like. Nowadays, a list of hurricane names is prepared before the start of each year.

Q How far ahead can forecasts predict the weather?

A They can predict about one week ahead. Past weather records are sometimes used to forecast weather further ahead, but this is very unreliable.

Q Are the television weather people real meteorologists?

A Not all of them are. Some are professional presenters who work from a weather center script. Others are scientists who do their own forecasts.

A weather station

Q Are there forecasts other than on television?

A Yes, lots of them. Forecasts are made for shipping, for aircraft, for road and rail travel, and even for large shops. There are also forecasts in newspapers and on the radio.

Q How do you become a weather expert?

A At school you would need to study maths and physics. In college you could study meteorology. Degrees in maths, oceanography and physics can also lead to a career in meteorology.

A halo around the Sun can be the sign of an approaching warm front. Rain may follow within 12 hours.

Can we predict the weather?

Although the most accurate predictions come from meteorologists, anyone can make local predictions by watching the sky and using simple equipment.

Q What equipment is it useful to have?

A A weather vane, thermometer, barometer and a rain gauge are all helpful.

Thermometer

Barometer

Q How can you measure wind?

A You can measure wind direction with a weather vane, and wind speed with the Beaufort scale (see page 8). Remember that wind direction is the direction that the wind is blowing from.

Weather vane

N E W S

Q What are the signs of showers?

A A dark cumulonimbus cloud may appear in the sky, especially on a spring or summer afternoon. Watch it carefully - if it's coming toward you, showers are probably on the way.

Dark cumulonimbus clouds are a sign of rain.

Q What are the signs of heavy, continuous rain on the way?

A A barometer will show a drop in air pressure and the sky will cloud over. High clouds, such as cirrostratus, will be replaced by thicker medium or low clouds.

Sheep's wool expands and uncurls when air is humid and can be used to predict bad weather.

closed

open

Pine cones are said to be good weather forecasters. In dry weather, their scales open; if they close it often means that rain is on the way.

Some people still believe that cows lie down when it is going to rain. However, scientists have studied many herds of cows and found that it is not true.

Q How can you measure rainfall?

A Use a simple homemade rain gauge. Stand a large dish or bucket in the middle of an open space, such as a lawn. Each day tip any rainwater in a measuring cup to measure the amount.

Q Is country weather lore ever reliable?

A For centuries country people have looked to the world around them for signs of the coming weather. Although a lot of so-called "country weather lore" is unreliable, some things in nature can give fairly accurate predictions. Seaweed is often used by natural weather forecasters. In dry weather it dries out and shrivels. If rain threatens it swells and feels damp to the touch.

Seaweed

Q What should you do with all your observations?

A Keep a record of all your observations in a weather diary. Make a note of cloud amount, wind direction and wind speed, and any rain or snow. If you have a barometer and thermometer, write down the pressure and temperature at the same time each day. You could also record the "state of the ground"- whether your lawn or backyard is wet, damp, dry, frosty or snowy.

Date
Temp
Pressure
Ground
7/25
71.5°F
1028
DRY

Exhaust fumes in our cities are one of the biggest problems. Electric cars and trains could be one solution.

Is our climate changing?

Scientists have estimated that by 2050, the Earth's temperature could have risen 5 - 11°F.

The world's climate is slowly changing, but we don't fully understand why. Thermometer readings show that it has grown more than one degree Fahrenheit warmer in the last 100 years.

Q Is today's climate very different to that of fifty-thousand years ago?

A Yes. Fifty-thousand years ago Earth was in the middle of the last Ice Age and much of the Earth's surface was covered in a thick sheet of ice. This ice age came to an end about 15,000 years ago when the climate started to get warmer and the ice melted. The age we now live in is called "interglacial."

Q Is the "Greenhouse Effect" a good thing?

A No. If the Greenhouse Effect continues, some countries will become too hot. Also, less rain will fall in some areas, and crops won't grow. Some scientists believe that if Earth becomes warmer, the Antarctic sheet will start to melt, flooding some low-lying areas.

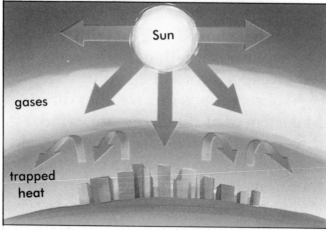

Sun

gases

trapped heat

Q What is the "Greenhouse Effect?"

A The "Greenhouse Effect" is caused by cars, factories and power stations releasing gases, particularly carbon dioxide, into the atmosphere. Like a greenhouse, these gases trap heat and gradually make the climate warmer.

Pollution is slowly damaging our planet.

Many people believe that unless humans stop polluting the Earth with CFCs and carbon dioxide, we could endanger all life on our planet.

Scientists and engineers are improving ways of capturing solar power and wind power. These methods of making electricity produce no waste gases.

Q What is the ozone layer?

A The ozone is a layer of gas very high in the atmosphere. This layer protects us from the Sun's harmful ultraviolet rays.

Q How can the destruction of the rainforests affect the weather?

A The world's rainforests are being cut down or burnt at a rate of around 9 sq. mi. per hour. If this continues it could lead to dramatic changes in rainfall and temperature patterns.

Q Is there a hole in the ozone layer?

A Although the ozone layer has become thin in many places, there are no actual holes in it. However, it is being destroyed by chemicals called chlorofluorocarbons (CFCs), which are used in aerosol sprays, and refridgerators.

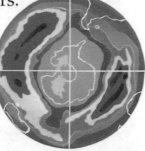

A satellite picture of Earth showing the thinning ozone layer.

Q Can we stop some of these climate changes?

A Yes, but it will need a big effort by everyone, especially in rich countries. You could do your part by conserving power and cutting down on ways you pollute the Earth. Switch lights off when you leave a room and put on an extra shirt rather than turn up the heat. Avoid using things that contain CFCs and walk or cycle for short journeys rather than travel in a car.

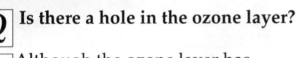

Scientists think that the Universe may contain huge amounts of invisible material called dark matter.

What is space?

S pace is the name we give to the region beyond our planet, Earth, which may stretch on forever. Space is made of nothing at all, but it has lots of things in it, such as planets and stars. Space and its contents are called the Universe.

Q How was the Universe made?

A Many scientists believe that the Universe is the result of an explosion called the Big Bang, which occurred about 14 billion years ago.

Q What was the Big Bang?

A The Big Bang was an explosion of all the matter in the Universe, which was squashed into a tiny area at more than 27 billion°F. The matter exploded so quickly that, within a hundredth of a second, the Universe was as big as the Sun! It continued to grow.

Q Is there anything left of the Big Bang?

A Scientists have found that the average temperature of the Universe is 8°F above absolute zero, which is the coldest temperature possible. This heat could come from the Big Bang continuing to slow down.

Absolute zero

Q Is the Universe still getting bigger?

A Yes. Scientists have discovered that matter and groups of stars are still moving further away from each other. However, they are now moving much more slowly than just after the Big Bang.

In 1929, Edwin Hubble discovered that the Universe was getting bigger. This led to the Big Bang theory.

Stars would explode if gravity were not holding their material together.

Q How do we measure large distances in space?

A Other stars and planets are so far away that if we measured the distance in miles, the number would be enormous. Instead, scientists measure these huge distances in light-years. Light travels at 186,000 mi. per second, so a light-year is the distance light travels in one year - 5,878,000,000,000 mi.!

Q What is the Universe made of?

A Everything in the Universe is made of atoms. When the Universe had cooled down after the Big Bang, tiny particles called protons, electrons and neutrons formed. These particles joined together in different ways to make up different sorts of atoms. For example, a helium atom is made up of two electrons, two protons and two neutrons.

Q How were stars and planets formed?

A Atoms have gravity, which means that they pull things toward them. After the Big Bang, gravity made atoms clump together to form stars and planets. Stars are made of hydrogen and helium atoms. Solid planets are made of carbon and iron atoms.

Q How big is the Universe?

A Scientists do not know how big the Universe is. So far, their instruments have been able to see as far as 300 million light-years into space, where there is a long line of galaxies. (A galaxy is a group of stars.) Scientists do not yet know what is beyond!

Scientists who study stars and planets are called astronomers.

What is a galaxy?

A galaxy is a group of millions of stars. A spiral galaxy looks like a huge, spinning Catherine wheel. Most of the stars are in the centre, with trailing spiral arms of stars around the outside.

Q What is the Milky Way?

A The Milky Way is the name of our galaxy. It is a spiral galaxy and our Solar System is in one of its spiral arms. The centre of the Milky Way can sometimes be spotted at night. It looks like a misty streak across the sky.

Q How many galaxies are there in the Universe?

A There may be 100 billion galaxies!

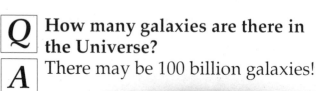

Q Which is the biggest galaxy?

A The Andromeda Galaxy is the biggest galaxy of those near the Milky Way. On a clear night, all you can see of this galaxy is a small fuzzy blob, but it has twice as many stars as the Milky Way - perhaps as many as 200 billion! There may be galaxies even bigger than Andromeda.

Q When were galaxies discovered?

A The first astronomers called misty patches in the sky nebulae, which means mist. It was not until early this century that it was found that many of these mysterious nebulae were actually distant galaxies.

The Milky Way measures about 588,000,000,000,000,000 mi., or 100,000 light years across.

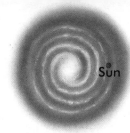

The ancient Greeks gave the Milky Way its name because they thought it was made of drops of milk from the breasts of the goddess Hera.

Q **What is at the centre of the Milky Way?**

A Scientists have discovered that there is a huge amount of hot gas at the centre of our galaxy. Some experts think that this may be caused by a enormous, swirling black hole which is slowly sucking in dust, gas and even light. You can find out more about black holes on page 175.

There are millions of spiral galaxies in the Universe. These galaxies contain many young stars.

Q **Are galaxies evenly spread throughout space?**

A There are enormous distances between galaxies, but scientists think that they are grouped in clusters. There may be thousands of galaxies in each cluster. Clusters of galaxies may, in turn, be grouped in superclusters.

Q **Are all galaxies shaped like the Milky Way?**

A No. Galaxies can also be shaped like barred spirals and ellipses. Other galaxies have no definite shape.

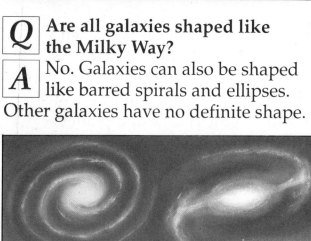

Spiral

Barred spiral

Elliptical

Irregular

Solar comes from the latin word "sol," which means sun.

What is a solar system?

Pluto is the most distant planet in our Solar System. It is over 3 billion mi. from Earth.

A solar system is a group of planets and moons which travel around, or orbit, a star. Every star is actually a sun, which may have its own solar system.

Q What are the planets in our Solar System called?

A The nine planets which orbit our Sun are called Mercury, Venus, Earth, Mars, Jupiter, Saturn, Uranus, Neptune and Pluto.

Q How old is the Solar System?

A Our Solar System was formed about 4.6 billion years ago, nearly 10 billion years after the Universe began. New stars and solar systems are still being formed!

Q How long does it take each planet to orbit the Sun?

A It takes Earth a year to travel once around the Sun. Planets nearer the Sun take less time and planets further away take longer. The table below shows how long it takes each planet to orbit the Sun.

Mercury	87.97	days
Venus	224.70	days
Earth	365.26	days
Mars	686.98	days
Jupiter	11.86	years
Saturn	29.50	years
Uranus	84.01	years
Neptune	164.79	years
Pluto	248.54	years

Q Can we see any planets from Earth without a telescope?

A The five planets nearest to Earth can be seen with the naked eye. These are Mercury, Venus, Mars, Jupiter and Saturn. They were first sighted in prehistoric times.

Saturn

Uranus

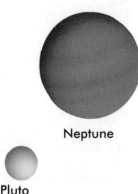

Neptune

Pluto

Ganymede is the biggest moon in our Solar System. It measures 3,268 mi. across and orbits Jupiter.

The planets in our Solar System are named after the Roman gods. Mars was the god of war.

Q What is the difference between a planet and a moon?

A Planets orbit suns, while moons orbit planets.

Q Are there any other planets in our Solar System beyond Pluto?

A So far, six tiny planets have been found. The first two have been named Smiley and Karla. Scientists once hoped that a large planet would be discovered, but now it seems unlikely.

Q Do other planets have moons?

A Yes. Most planets have moons. Saturn has 19 moons, Jupiter and Uranus have 16 each, Neptune has 6, Mars has 2 and Pluto has only 1 moon.

Here you can see the Sun and planets in our Solar System (not to scale).

Jupiter

Mars

Earth

Venus

Mercury

Sun

What is the Sun?

Before clocks were invented, people used sundials to tell what time of day it was.

The Sun is a star. It is a great, glowing ball of hydrogen and helium gas. Without the Sun's light and heat, nothing could survive on Earth.

Q How hot is the Sun?

A The Sun is very hot indeed! Its surface is 16,394°F, and the temperature at the center measures 38 million°F!

Q Is Earth bigger than the Sun?

A No. Although, the Sun looks quite small to us, it is actually one million times bigger than our planet, Earth.

 Earth ⟵ The Sun is 92,961,000 mi. from Earth. ⟶ Sun

Q How do the Sun's rays affect Earth?

A Without the Sun's rays, life on Earth would die. Plants need the Sun's light to change carbon dioxide and water into the food they need. In turn, humans and animals rely on plants for their food supply.

Sunspots are cooler areas on the Sun's surface. Some are bigger than Earth.

This is a close-up view of the Sun.

A white dwarf star is a star that has used up its hydrogen fuel.

White dwarf

You must NEVER use a telescope or binoculars to look directly at the Sun - its light could blind you.

Q Will the Sun last for ever?

A It will last for many millions of years! In about 5 billion years' time, the Sun will have burnt up all of its hydrogen fuel. It will become a hundred times as bright as it is now, and swell up to swallow the nearest planets, including Earth. After another 100 million years, the Sun will shrink to become a white dwarf star.

Solar flares are huge clouds of glowing gases which loop above the Sun's surface.

Q Is the Sun moving?

A Yes. All the planets in our Solar System orbit the Sun and, in turn, our Solar System orbits the center of our galaxy, the Milky Way. It takes about 225 million years, or one cosmic year, for the Sun and nine planets to travel around the Milky Way once.

The Sun in the Milky Way (not to scale)

Q Can the Sun's rays be harmful?

A We receive the Sun's light and heat, but most of the dangerous rays, such as ultra violet rays, are stopped by the layers of gas in Earth's atmosphere. However, the ozone layer is getting thinner. Scientists believe that it is being damaged by chemicals from Earth.

---------- The ozone layer

Q Can spacecraft get close to the Sun?

A The Sun is so hot that spacecraft cannot fly very near it. In 1976 *Helios 2* traveled to within 28,000,000 mi. of the Sun. This is closer than the Sun's nearest planet, Mercury.

Helios 2

Venus is always surrounded by clouds of sulphuric acid.

What are planets made of?

Venus

Like Earth, most of the smaller planets in our Solar System have a solid surface made of rock. However, the four biggest planets (Jupiter, Saturn, Uranus and Neptune) are made of gases!

Q Could we breathe on any other planet in our Solar System?

A No. One of Saturn's moons, Titan, may have an atmosphere made of nitrogen gas (which makes up four-fifths of Earth's atmosphere). However, to stay alive, human beings also need oxygen.

Q Is there life on other planets?

A All of the planets in the Solar System have been explored, using telescopes and space probes. So far, nothing living has been found. The other planets in our system all seem to be too hot, too cold, or made entirely of gases.

Q Are there mountains, valleys and volcanoes on other planets?

A Yes, most solid planets have geographical features like Earth. Scientists have found deserts, polar areas, mountains and valleys on Mars. Volcanoes have been found on Venus, Mars and Io (one of Jupiter's moons). The biggest volcano of all is on Mars. It is called Mount Olympus and it is 15 mi. high!

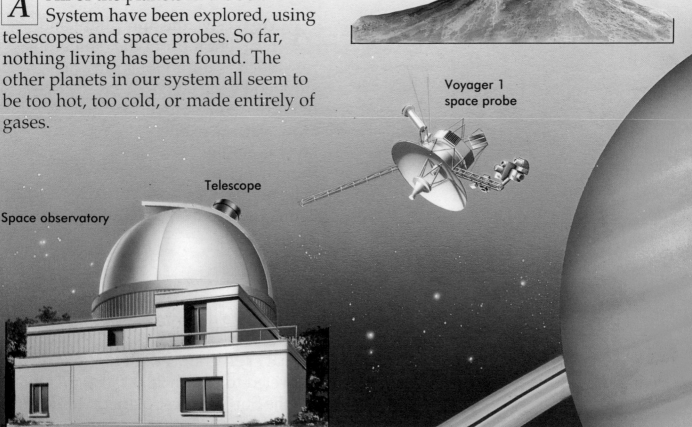

Voyager 1 space probe

Telescope

Space observatory

The Great Red Spot on Jupiter's surface is actually a furious storm.

Saturn's rings can be spotted even with a small telescope.

Q **Why is Mars red?**

A Mars is red because it is rusty! The surface of the planet is covered in iron oxide, or rust, which forms when iron mixes with small amounts of oxygen and water.

Q **Why does Saturn have stripes?**

A Saturn's atmosphere is made of different gases. Some of these gases do not mix and when Saturn spins, high winds blow the gas around the planet into stripes. Each stripe is a different mixture of gas.

Q **What shape are planets?**

A A planet may look round, but it is are shaped like an ellipse. This means that it looks like a squashed ball. Saturn and Jupiter spin very quickly so they are the most squashed planets.

Saturn's rings

Saturn

Q **What are Saturn's rings made of?**

A Saturn's rings are made of millions of particles of dust and ice. There are so many of them in orbit around Saturn that it makes the rings look solid. The rings shine because the ice particles in them reflect light.

Could people live on the Moon?

An astronaut last walked on the Moon in 1973.

There is no atmosphere on the Moon, so you would not be able to breathe. It is possible to set up scientific bases there, but anyone walking around on the Moon would need a space suit.

Q Why is the Moon covered in craters?

A Most of the Moon's craters were caused about three billion years ago by meteorites. These lumps of rock and iron hurled through Space and crashed into the Moon at high speed.

Q What are the dark areas on the Moon?

A When people first looked through telescopes at the Moon, they thought that the dark areas were seas. They gave them names, such as the Sea of Tranquility. It was later discovered that these seas were really areas of dry, dark lava from volcanic eruptions.

Q Why isn't Earth covered with craters ?

A Earth was once covered with craters, but most have been worn away by rain, wind and movement of the Earth's crust. There is no weather on the Moon, so its craters have not been worn away.

The Moon is bigger than the planet Pluto.

Moon

Pluto

The Moon is about 238,866 mi. from Earth. It would take you more than 9 years to walk there!

Q What is an eclipse of the Sun?

A This occurs when the Moon is directly between Earth and the Sun. For a few moments, the Sun's light is blocked and the Moon casts a shadow onto Earth, turning day into night!

An eclipse of the Sun

Q What happens when there is an eclipse of the Moon?

A This occurs when Earth is directly between the Moon and the Sun. We can only see the Moon because it reflects the Sun's light. If Earth travels between the Sun and the Moon, it stops the Sun's light from reaching the Moon, so the Moon seems to disappear.

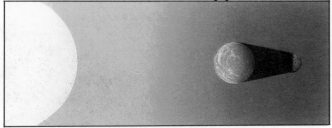

Q Why does the Moon seem to change shape?

A The Sun's light only falls on one side of the Moon. It takes 27.3 days or one lunar month, for the Moon to orbit Earth. As the Moon orbits Earth, we see different amounts of the sunlit side of the Moon. When we can see all of the sunlit side, there is a full moon.

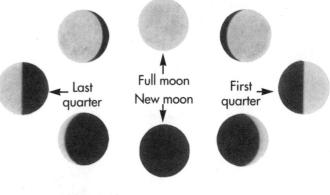

Last quarter

Full moon
New moon

First quarter

Q Does the Moon affect Earth?

A Yes, the Moon has its own gravity, which pulls Earth's seas toward it, making them bulge. As the Earth spins, the bulge moves around its surface. When the Moon is overhead, the sea reaches its highest level. When the Moon is over the coast, there is a high tide.

The Sun's gravity also has a small effect on Earth's seas. When the Sun and Moon both pull at once, there is a very high tide. This is called a spring tide.

The word comet means "hairy star."

What is an asteroid belt?

There are thousands of pieces of rock, called asteroids, in orbit around the Sun. Most of these asteroids are grouped together between Mars and Jupiter. These large groups of rocks are known as asteroid belts.

Q What are comets made of?

A Comets are huge balls of shining, frozen rock, gas and dust. The comet has a tail made of gas and dust which blows out from it in the solar wind sent out by the Sun. There may be as many as 100 billion comets orbiting the Sun.

Q How big are comets?

A The Giotto Space Probe showed that the head of Halley's Comet was as large as a mountain. A comet's tail can be over 62 million mi. long!

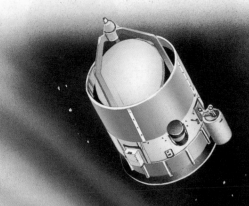

Q How did Halley's Comet get its name?

A In the 1600s, the brilliant scientist Edmond Halley realized that one particular comet orbited the Sun every 76 years. He correctly predicted that its next appearance would be in 1758. It will next be seen in 2062.

When lots of dust hits Earth's atmosphere, it burns up, and looks like lots of shooting stars. This is called a meteor shower.

A meteorite is a meteor that has fallen to Earth.

Q Did an asteroid kill the last of the dinosaurs?

A Perhaps. An asteroid which might have been as large as 6 mi. across fell near Yucatan, in Mexico, about 65 million years ago. The Chicxlub Crater made by this asteroid is 112 mi. across. The force of the blast caused tidal waves and earthquakes and threw huge clouds of dust into the sky. Scientists think that all land animals that weighed over 66 lbs. died, including the last of the dinosaurs.

Q What are shooting stars?

A Shooting stars are not stars at all! They are actually tiny pieces of dust, called meteors. When a comet flies past, dust from its burning tail falls toward Earth. When these particles of dust hit Earth's atmosphere at very high speed, they burn up. On Earth, this looks as if a star is falling from the sky.

Q Which is the biggest asteroid in our solar system?

A Asteroids are bigger than meteors and are like small planets. The largest asteroid in our Solar System is Ceres, which is over 621 mi. wide.

The force of the meteorite explosion in Siberia created such strong winds, that a farmer 124 mi. away was almost blown over.

Q When was the last time a large meteor hit Earth?

A The last time this happened was in 1908 in a remote area of Siberia, Russia. Great areas of trees were knocked down by the blast.

Why do stars twinkle?

The nearest star to our Sun is Proxima Centauri, which is 4.3 light-years or 25,277 billion mi. away.

Stars twinkle because the light they send toward Earth is bent by air currents moving around in our atmosphere. If you were to travel above Earth's atmosphere, the stars would not twinkle at all!

Q Why do stars shine?

A Stars shine because they are hot, just like our Sun. Inside a star, hydrogen gas turns into helium gas, which gives out energy in the form of light, heat and other invisible rays.

Q Can we tell the time by the stars?

A Yes. Earth spins around once every 24 hours. During the night, stars appears to move across the sky. It is possible to tell the time when their changing positions are measured. Before clocks, stars were an important way of telling the time at night.

Q Where is the best place to see stars?

A Bright stars can be seen easily from anywhere on clear nights, but the best place to see the dimmer stars is in the countryside. In towns, artificial light from street lighting fills the sky, making it difficult to see the dimmer stars.

The Sun is so far away that its light takes 8 minutes to reach us on Earth.

A star is formed in our galaxy every 18 days. That means there are 20 new stars each year!

Q What is the best time of night to see stars?

A The best time to see stars is when the sky is at its darkest. This is at midnight, when the Sun is on the opposite side of Earth.

Q Can we measure a star's brightness?

A Yes. A star's brightness is called its magnitude. A star of magnitude 0 is very bright. Stars of magnitude 5 are only just visible. Really bright stars have minus magnitudes. Sirius, the brightest star in the sky, has a magnitude of -1.5.

Q How did sailors use the stars to find their way at night ?

A If you live in the northern hemisphere, one star seems to stay still. This is called the Pole Star as it is almost directly over the North Pole. Sailors knew that its position showed the north, so they could then work out in which direction to sail.

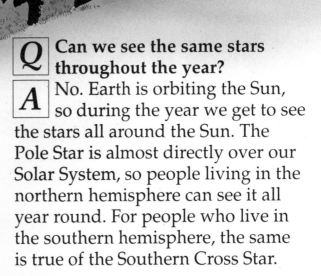

Q Can we see the same stars throughout the year?

A No. Earth is orbiting the Sun, so during the year we get to see the stars all around the Sun. The Pole Star is almost directly over our Solar System, so people living in the northern hemisphere can see it all year round. For people who live in the southern hemisphere, the same is true of the Southern Cross Star.

Sun

How are stars formed?

The Sun is a yellow star. Its surface temperature is 16,394°F.

Stars form when hydrogen atoms in space are attracted to each other and clump together. The gas begins to burn and the star shines.

Q How long do stars last?

A The larger a star is, the shorter its life will be. Our Sun is quite small compared with some stars and has a life-span of 10 billion years. Really large stars only last for a few million years.

Q Are stars the same color?

A No. If you look closely at stars, they are different colors. A star's color depends on its temperature. Blue stars are the hottest. Red stars are cooler. Here are some stars and their approximate surface temperatures:

Red	up to 11,000°F
Orange	about 14,000°F
Yellow	15,000 - 21,000°F
White	21,000 - 27,000°F
Blue-white	27,000 - 54,000°F
Blue	54,000 - 135,000°F

Q What is a supernova?

A A supernova is a huge star which has blown up after running out of fuel. After it explodes, the star collapses and debris is flung into space to form new stars and planets. All that is left of the supernova is a small neutron star.

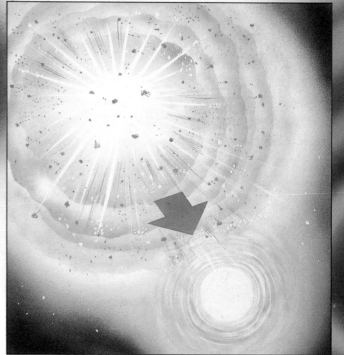

Q What is a pulsar?

A A pulsar is a spinning neutron star, left behind after a large supernova explosion. It is called a pulsar because of the pulses, or flashes of energy, it sends out as it spins.

Some nebulae are made from debris left behind after supernovae have exploded (right).

Red stars are the dimmest. They are the most difficult to see.

Q What is a black hole?

A When a really large star explodes into a supernovae, a strange thing happens. The star collapses so much that all of the material in it is squashed together. This squashed star has so much gravity that it attracts other material, even light, toward it and sucks it all in, so that it can never escape. This is called a black hole.

Black hole

Q What is a white dwarf star?

A At the end of their lifetimes, some smaller stars become very big and bright, before shrinking into white dwarf stars. Eventually, these white dwarf stars cool down and fade away.

Q What are quasars?

A Quasars are tiny star-like objects far away in space. We can only see them because they give out so much energy. Astronomers are still not sure exactly what they are!

Q What are wandering stars?

A Wandering stars are actually planets. We can see five planets - Mercury, Venus, Mars, Jupiter and Saturn - from Earth without a telescope. These planets look as if they are wandering around in the sky.

Two astronomers used Newton's laws to predict the existence of Neptune. They were proven right when it was later seen in 1846.

Who were the first astronomers?

Neptune

T he Ancient Greeks were the first scientific astronomers. They worked out the size of Earth and that there were enormous distances between our Sun and other stars.

Q When were telescopes invented?

A Telescopes were invented at the end of the 1500s. Galileo Galilei, an Italian astronomer, was the first to use a telescope to look at the night sky. At that time, many people believed that the Sun orbited Earth. Galileo was condemned by the church for saying that the Sun, not Earth, was the center of the Solar System. He was, of course, correct!

Galileo Galilei

Q What is a radio telescope?

A Some objects cannot be seen with an optical telescope, but the radio waves that they give out can be detected with a radio telescope. Karl Jansky built the first radio telescope in 1932.

Radio telescope

Q What is the electromagnetic spectrum?

A The electromagnetic spectrum is the range of all the energy we know about in the Universe. It stretches from wide radio waves to narrow gamma rays. Stars give out different amounts of each type of energy. This information can be recorded as a sort of bar code, called an emission spectrum. Scientists use this information to find out what materials a star is made of.

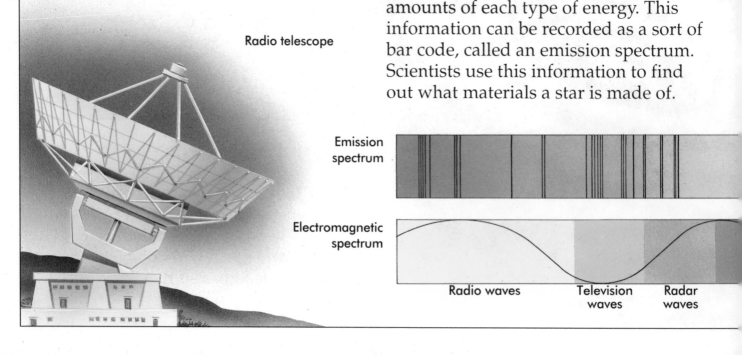

Emission spectrum

Electromagnetic spectrum

Radio waves   Television waves   Radar waves

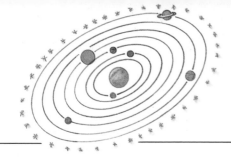

Ptolemy was a famous early astronomer who worked in Egypt. He thought that the Sun, the Moon, planets and stars in our Solar System orbited Earth.

177

Q How does a refractor telescope work?

A A refractor telescope uses a curved lens to bend and magnify light from distant objects, such as stars.

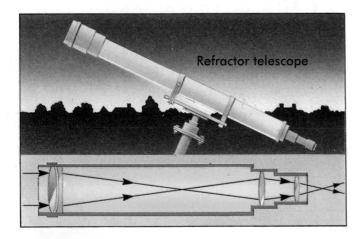

Refractor telescope

Q How does a reflector telescope work?

A This telescope bends light with mirrors. It was invented by scientist Isaac Newton in 1668.

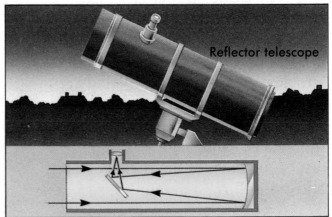

Reflector telescope

Q Which is the most powerful optical telescope in the world?

A This is a reflecting telescope with a mirror that measures 19 ft. across. It weighs 78 tons and is housed at the Zlenchukskya Observatory in the Russian Caucasus Mountains. The Keck telescope in Hawaii is bigger, but this is made up of several hexagonal mirrors joined together like a honeycomb.

If a color appears on a star's emission spectrum, that star is giving out a particular type of energy. Black lines show that some types of energy are missing.

Q Who discovered gravity?

A Sir Isaac Newton discovered the force of gravity in 1665. Gravity is a pulling force that keeps the stars and planets in their orbits. Earth's gravity stops the Moon from floating away into space. The Sun's gravity keeps all the planets in our Solar System in orbit around it.

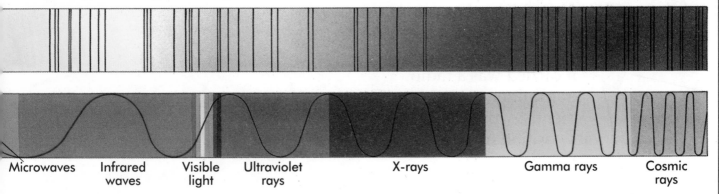

Microwaves   Infrared waves   Visible light   Ultraviolet rays   X-rays   Gamma rays   Cosmic rays

The Space Shuttle orbits Earth at 17,400 mph.

Earth's gravity is so strong that rockets are needed to propel satellites and other spacecraft out of the atmosphere and into space.

Q How does a rocket work?

A If a balloon is filled with air and then released, it speeds along - a rocket works in the same way. A mixture of hydrogen and oxygen fuel explodes all the time, pushing hot gas out of the back of the rocket and propelling it along.

Q What are satellites?

A Satellites are space vehicles which orbit our planet. They can relay television, radio and telephone signals around Earth. Some satellites give us weather forecasts, and others look for evidence of resources, such as oil, hidden beneath Earth's surface.

Q Which was the first satellite?

A The first satellite was *Sputnik 1*, launched in Russia on October 4, 1957. It stayed in orbit for only 90 days. The only equipment that it carried was a radio transmitter, so that scientists could track its position from Earth.

Sputnik 1

Q What happens to rockets after launching a spacecraft?

A Rockets are only needed for the first few seconds of a spacecraft's journey. They then fall back down to Earth, land in the sea and are recovered by special ships.

The fuel tank holds 1 million gallons of fuel to power the orbiter's own rockets.

The rocket boosters give the Shuttle extra push for the lift-off. They fall off only 30 seconds into the flight.

A spacecraft has to travel at 28,856 mph to escape Earth's atmosphere.

Some satellites always stay above the same part of Earth. These are usually weather satellites.

There are heat-resistant tiles on the Orbiter that stop it from bursting into flames when it re-enters Earth's atmosphere.

For the launch, the Orbiter is attached to the fuel tank and boosters for the launch. It needs no fuel to glide back to Earth after its mission.

The Orbiter's rockets give most of the power to push it out of Earth's atmosphere

Q **How do spacecraft land back on Earth safely?**

A Spacecraft such as *Apollo* and *Soyuz* both land in the sea when they come back to Earth. However, the Space Shuttle is specially designed to land like a normal airplane on a runway.

Q **Can spacecraft be reused?**

A Until 1981, all spacecraft were only used once, but new types of craft such as the American Space Shuttle and the Russian *Buran* Shuttle can be used over and over again.

Q **Where are spacecraft built?**

A American spacecraft, such as the Space Shuttle and *Saturn V*, are built in the largest scientific building in the world. This is the Vehicle Assembly Building (VAB) at the Kennedy Space Center in Florida. The VAB's doors are 460 ft. high, so spacecraft can be rolled out.

Vehicle Assembly Building, Florida

Who were the first astronauts?

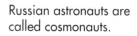

Yuri Gagarin from Russia was the first man in space on April 12, 1961. In 1963, Valentina Tereshkova became the first woman to be launched into space.

Q How many astronauts have been to the Moon?

A A total of twelve astronauts have landed on the Moon in spacecraft called *Apollo 11, 12, 14, 15, 16* and *17*. Unfortunately, *Apollo 13* had many technical problems and its lunar module was unable to land. The crew had to fly the damaged spacecraft using the stars' positions as a guide. They landed safely back on Earth.

Q What was the first living thing to go into space?

A A dog called Lemonchik (meaning "little lemon") was the first living being to go into space. It was launched on the *Sputnik 2* mission. Unfortunately, it died when the oxygen ran out.

Q What is a space station?

A A space station is a large spacecraft which stays in orbit around Earth. Scientists can live and work there for long periods of time. The Russian *Mir* Space Station was launched in 1986.

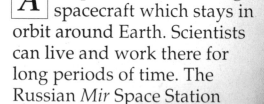

Q How do astronauts train?

A Astronauts have special training to prepare them for the feeling of weightlessness in space. Before their flight, astronauts often rehearse space experiments and missions underwater. A swimming pool is filled with very salty water, which makes the astronauts float as if they were in space.

In space, weightlessness makes it very difficult to eat meals off plates. Instead, astronauts suck food out of tubes.

Without the pull of Earth's gravity, people become about $^3/_4$ in. taller in space!

Q What do astronauts do in space?

A There is no air in space, so astronauts are able to carry out experiments which cannot be done on Earth. Rather than bring satellites back to Earth for repairs, astronauts can make adjustments in space. In 1993, the Hubble Space Telescope was successfully repaired in orbit by astronauts from the Space Shuttle.

Q How are space stations sent into space?

A Although early space stations could be launched on one rocket, they are now so big that they have to be sent into space piece by piece.

Q Can space make astronauts ill?

A When astronauts stay in space for long periods of time, lack of exercise and weightlessness can affect them - bones lose calcium and muscles become weak. Without the protection of Earth's atmosphere, astronauts may be affected by harmful rays from the Sun.

The American space agency is called N.A.S.A. This stands for National Aeronautics and Space Administration.

How can you find out more?

Visiting a planetarium, joining an astronomy club or looking round a science museum are just a few of the ways you can find out more about space.

Q Are there plans for any more space stations?

A Yes. An American space station called "Freedom" is planned, but the enormous cost means that the project has been postponed several times. If *Freedom* ever does get off the ground, it will probably link up with the Russian *Mir* space station, allowing Russian and American astronauts to work together in space.

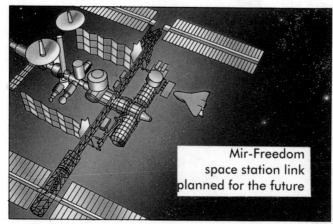

Mir-Freedom space station link planned for the future

Q How far have spacecraft travelled into space?

A The *Pioneer 10* space probe has travelled the furthest distance. It flew past Pluto in 1986 and is still heading out into deep space!

Pioneer 10 space probe

Q How can we see further into space?

A Earth's atmosphere blocks out many of the rays which come from distant objects in the Universe. The Hubble Space Telescope was sent above the atmosphere so that scientists could have a clearer view and see further into space. Other instruments, such as radio telescopes, could also be sent into space to find out more about the Universe.

Pluto

Captain John Young has been into space more than anyone else. He has flown on 6 space flights.

One of the next planned space mission is a trip to Mars. N.A.S.A. hopes to send astronauts there in the next 50 years.

Q **Have we received any messages from space?**

A Not yet! Scientists have been listening for messages from space for years, but so far none have been received. As far as we know, signals can only be sent at the speed of light. If there were alien beings in other solar systems, they would be so far away that any messages we received from them would be thousands or even millions of years old by the time they reached us.

Q **Can anyone be an astronaut?**

A When space travel first began, astronauts were all specially trained airplane pilots. Now, however, astronauts can be experts from different sciences who are sent into space to carry out experiments. However, competition is so fierce that as well as being science experts, hopeful astronauts also have to be lucky enough to be chosen!

Q **What messages have been sent to space?**

A Yes, in 1977, two probes called *Pioneer 10* and *Pioneer 11* were launched into space. They each carried a plaque (see below) with information about our planet. Each plaque showed pictures of human beings and also space maps which gave directions to the Sun and showed the position of Earth in our Solar System.

Message on board Pioneer probes

Q **How do you become an astronomer?**

A Anyone can study the night sky! You can stargaze from your back garden and even a small telescope gives a better view of the stars. Astronomers usually study astronomy, mathematics, physics or another science at university, and work in observatories around the world as part of their training.

The oldest dinosaur bones found so far belong to Eoraptor which lived 228 million years ago.

Test your knowledge

Tyrannosaurus rex's name means "king of the dinosaurs."

DINOSAURS

Q What was a therapod?

A Therapods were two-legged meat-eating dinosaurs, like Tyrannosaurus rex.

Q Were baby dinosaurs born or did they hatch from eggs?

A Most scientists think that all dinosaurs hatched from eggs.

Q Why did the dinosaurs die out?

A A popular explanation is that they died because of high temperatures caused by a meteorite explosion.

Q Are any of today's animals descendants of dinosaurs?

A Yes. Birds are descendants of dinosaurs!

Q Did herbivorous dinosaurs eat grass?

A No. Grass did not grow on Earth until after the dinosaurs had become extinct.

Q What does dinosaur mean?

A Dinosaur means "terrible lizard!".

Q Which dinosaurs had the smallest brains?

A A stegosaur's brain was only as big as a walnut.

Q Where are dinosaur fossils found?

A Fossils are usually found in rocks which were formed under rivers, seas and oceans.

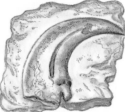

Q Who discovered the first dinosaur?

A Gideon Mantell, an English doctor, found Iguanodon teeth in 1822.

Q How long were Tyrannosaurus rex's teeth?

A They were more than 6 in. long!

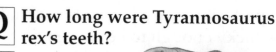
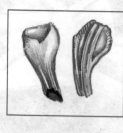

From a standing start, a cheetah can reach 44 mph in two seconds. It may have a top speed of 69 mph!

Plants give off oxygen which humans and animals must breathe in order to live.

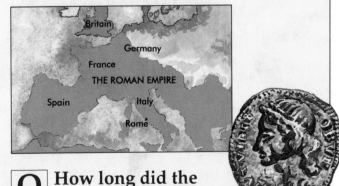

ANCIENT TIMES

Q What were hieroglyphs?

A These were pictures which were used to represent objects and sounds. The Ancient Egyptians wrote in hieroglyphs.

Q Who invented the wheelbarrow?

A Wheelbarrows were first used by the Chinese. They did not appear in Europe until 1,000 years later.

Q When did people migrate from Asia to the American mainland?

A This happened about 30,000 years ago. The first advanced civilizations grew up in Central America.

Q Who were the first people to have bathrooms?

A The Egyptians.

Q How were Egyptian craftsmen paid?

A Instead of receiving money, they were paid with food, linen, firewood and salt!

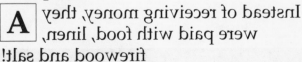

Q How long is the Great Wall of China?

A It is 2,150 mi. long!

Q Who was Hippocrates?

A Hippocrates was a Greek who became one of the first and most famous doctors.

Q Where was the Roman Empire?

A The Roman Empire included England, Wales, Mediterranean Europe and North Africa.

Britain
Germany
France
THE ROMAN EMPIRE
Spain
Italy
Rome

Q How long did the Roman Empire last?

A It lasted for over 1,000 years before finally ending in A.D.395.

America is named after an explorer called Amerigo Vespucci.

Test your knowledge

For 180 days a year, the North Pole and the South Pole get no sunlight at all.

EXPLORERS

Q Where did the Vikings come from?

A Groups of Vikings came from Denmark, Norway and Sweden.

Q What were longships?

A Longships were Viking warships. They were ideal for both raiding and long-distance travel.

Q Who was Marco Polo?

A Marco Polo was the first person to travel the entire length of the Silk Route – the famous Chinese\Asian trading route.

Q When was America discovered and by whom?

A Christopher Columbus never actually set foot in North America, but he is acknowledged as discovering the continent in 1492.

Q Who was Ferdinand Magellan?

A He led the first successful expedition to sail around the world in 1519. He was killed on the voyage, but one ship and 18 crew arrived back in 1522.

Q When were the North and South Poles first reached?

A Robert Peary reached the North Pole in 1909 and Roald Amundsen was the first to reach the South Pole in 1911.

PLANET EARTH

Q Which is the deepest part of the Earth?

A The Marianas Trench, a valley at the bottom of the Pacific Ocean is 36,202 ft. deep.

Chalk is made from the skeletons of tiny sea creatures and crustaceans.

There are about 500 active volcanoes in the world. Between 20 and 30 errupt every year. Most are under the sea.

PLANET EARTH

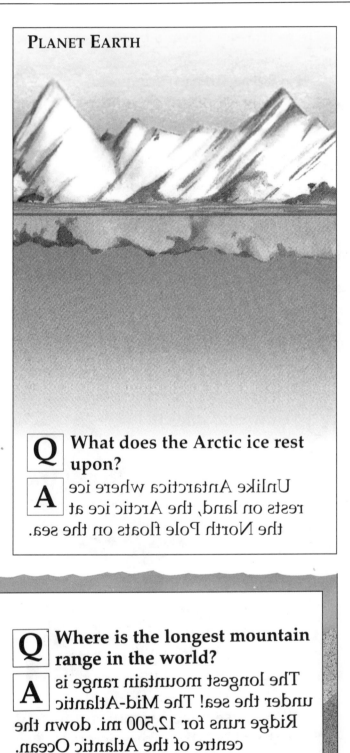

Q What does the Arctic ice rest upon?

A Unlike Antarctica where ice rests on land, the Arctic ice at the North Pole floats on the sea.

Q Where is the longest mountain range in the world?

A The longest mountain range is under the sea! The Mid-Atlantic Ridge runs for 12,500 mi. down the centre of the Atlantic Ocean.

Q How much of the Earth's surface is covered by oceans and seas?

A About seven-tenths of the Earth's surface is covered by water.

Q What do copper, quartz, rubies and diamonds have in common?

A They are all minerals – non-living substances found in the Earth.

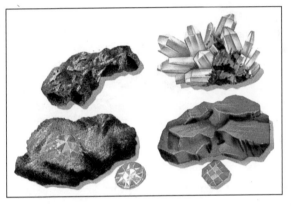

Q Which is the driest place in the world?

A Until 1971, it had not rained in South America's Atacama Desert for 400 years.

Q Which is the coldest part of the world?

A Antarctica is by far the coldest place on Earth.

Q How fast do glaciers move?

A Most glaciers move at less than 12 in. a day, but some travel at around 80 ft. a day.

When they are in motion at sea, large oil tankers can take up to 3.7 miles to stop.

Test your knowledge

The fastest racing power boats can travel at speeds of over 143 mph.

THE SEA

Q Is the sea always blue?

A No. The sea mirrors the color of the sky, so it can look dark gray in a storm.

Q Where is the Great Barrier Reef?

A The Great Barrier Reef is the near the north-east coast of Australia. It is the longest coral reef in the world.

THE WEATHER

Q What type of clouds are cumulonimbus?

A Cumulonimbus are low, dark, storm clouds.

Q How is wind strength measured?

A The Beaufort Scale is a way of measuring wind. Force 1 is a very light breeze. Force 8 is a strong gale.

Q Which is the wettest place in the world?

A The wettest recorded place is Mawsynram in India. It has 475 in. of rain per year.

Q How cold does it have to be to snow?

A The heaviest snowfalls occur when the temperature is around 32°F.

Q Where does lightning usually strike?

A Lightning tends to strike high places first, such as trees and towers.

Q Why is seaweed important to natural weather forecasters?

A Some forecasters claim they can use seaweed to predict the weather. If rain threatens it swells and feels damp.

A constellation is a named pattern of stars. Some constellations were named over 4,000 years ago.

A planisphere is a star chart that shows you which stars are in the sky on any night of the year.

Q What is a groyne?

A A groyne is a type of fence which divides a beach and stops sand and stones from being washed away.

Q Where might you find starfish, limpets, periwinkles or crabs?

A All of these creatures live in rock pools on the seashore.

Q Which creature has the biggest eyes?

A The giant squid has the biggest eyes. They measure 16 in. across.

Q What is a tsunami?

A It is a giant wave caused by earthquakes and volcanic eruptions under the sea.

SPACE

Q Which planet in our Solar System is furthest from the Sun?

A Pluto is furthest away from the Sun. It is 3 billion mi. from Earth!

Q Which is the highest mountain in the Universe?

A Mount Olympus is a volcano on Mars. It is 15.5 mi. high!

Q How big is the Sun?

A The Sun is one million times bigger than the Earth.

Q How old is the Universe?

A Scientists think that the Universe was formed 14 billion years ago.

Q Which is the hottest type of star?

A Blue stars are the hottest. They measure 55,000°F – 137,000°F.

Q How fast do spacecraft travel as they orbit Earth?

A Spacecraft travel at 17,400 mph as they orbit our planet.

Index

Aborigines 78-79
Abu Simbel 47
Acid rain 106, 132
Adulis 41
Africa 40-41, 54, 80-81
Air 24-25, 86, 106, 110, 124, 132
Air mass 126
Air pollution 106, 132
Air pressure 136-137, 152
Akkad 33
Aksum 41
Alexander the Great 49, 61
Aliens 183
Allosaurus 16-17
Altocumulus 140
Altostratus 140
Ammonite 30
Amundsen, Roald 82-83
Anatolia 33
Anchisaurus 9
Andromeda Galaxy 160
Anemometer 138
Ankylosaurs 4, 17
Antarctic sheet 152
Antarctica 96, 98-99 100-101, 106, 120, 122-123, 132
Apatosaurus 4, 10, 14, 16, 17, 22
Apollo spacecraft 180
Arabs 63, 66-67, 81
Archaeopteryx 18-19
Arctic 100
Assur 33
Assyrians 33, 43
Asteroids 170-171
Astrolabe 63
Astronauts 180-181, 183
Astronomers 160, 183
Athens 48-50
Atmosphere 106
Atmosphere 124-125, 126, 132, 134, 157, 163, 166, 171, 172, 181, 182
Atmospheric pressure 125, 126
Atoms 104, 130, 159
Australia 78-79
Axis 85, 109
Aztecs 76-77
Babylon 52
Balloons 152
Barometer 135-136, 154-155
Barosaurus 24
Barth, Heinrich 81

Baryonyx 26, 27
Batuta, Ibn 66
Beaches 91, 115
Beaufort Scale 138, 154
Belemnite 30
Big Bang 158-159
Black holes 161, 175
Blaxland, John 79
Blizzards 145
Brachiosaurus 7, 11, 16
Britannia 56
Brontosaur 17
Burke, Robert 79
Buys Ballot's Law 137
Cabot, John 71
Caesar, Julius 55
Camarasaurus 12, 15
Caravels 71
Carbon dioxide 106, 132, 156
Carthage 40, 54
Çatal Hüyük 32
Ceratopsians 4, 5, 12, 20
Ceratosaurus 14
CFCs 107, 132, 157
Charts 63
Chasmosaurus 21
Cheng, Emperor 36
China 68-69
Chinese 63, 68, 69, 73
Cirrocumulus 140
Cirrostratus 140, 154
Cirrus 140
Cities 102, 128
Clapperton, Hugh 81
Cliffs 90, 114
Climate 102-103, 128-129 134, 149
Climatologists 134
Clouds 88, 112, 126-127, 140, 141, 142
Clusters 161
Coal 104, 130
Coastal marshes 91, 115
Coastline 90, 114
Coelophysis 13, 21
Columbus, Christopher 71, 72-73
Comets 170
Compasses 63
Compsognathus 10, 17, 19
Coniferous forests 103, 129
Conquistadors 76-77
Continents 86, 100, 110
Cook, James 78

Coral reef 89, 113
Cortes, Hernando 76-77
Cosmonauts 181
Crab nebula 175
Craters 168
Crust 86, 88, 110, 112
Cumulonimbus 141, 145, 147, 154
Cumulus 140
Cuneiform 33
Damascus 32
Day 85, 97, 109, 121
Deltas 94, 118
Denham, Dixon 81
Deserts 96-97, 102, 120-121, 128
Dhows 66-67
Dias, Bartolomeo 70-71
Dinosaurs 171
Diplodocus 4-5, 10, 11, 12, 13, 22, 27
Dome mountains 92, 116
Drake, Francis 75, 77
Drought 143
Dryosaurus 14
Earth 162-163
Earth's axis 135
Earthquakes 86, 110
Eclipses 169
Egypt 33, 40-47, 52, 58
Egyptians 61
El Nino 150
Elasmosaur 17
Electricity 104, 130, 139, 144, 146
Electromagnetic spectrum 176-177
Emission spectrum 176-177
Eoraptor 5
Epidaurus 53
Equator 85, 102-103, 109, 127, 128-129, 142
Ethiopia 40-41
Etruscans 54
Euoplocephalus 12
Evaporation 148
Exhaust fumes 156
Exosphere 124
Faults 86, 110
Fish 105, 131
Fishbourne Villa 59
Flinders, Matthew 79
Floods 143
Fog 148, 149
Food crops 105, 131

Forecasts 152
Fossil fuels 104, 130
Freedom Space Station 182
Frost 145, 149
Gagarin, Yuri 180
Galaxies 160-161
Gales 148-149
Galilei, Galileo 176
Gallimimus 25
Gama, Vasco da 70, 71, 72
Ganymede 163
Gas 104-105, 130-131
Gaseous planets 170-171
Gaul 56
Giza 46
Glaciers 95, 98-99, 100, 119, 122-123
Global warming 106, 132
Goddess Hera 161
Gravity 84-85, 88, 91, 108, 109, 112, 115, 124, 135, 160, 169, 177, 178, 181
Great Age of Exploration 70-71
Great Wall of China 36
Greece 33, 48-53, 58
Greeks 43, 48-53, 57
Greenhouse effect 156
Groynes 90, 114
Guatemala 38
Hadrian's Wall 59
Hadrosaurs 4
Hailstones 145
Halley's Comet 170
Harappa 34
Hieroglyphics 47
Helios II 165
Hills 89, 113
Hittites 33
Hubble, Edwin 159
Hubble Space Telescope 181, 182
Humidity 142, 149, 152
Hurricanes 127
Hypsilophodon 15
Ice 94, 98, 100, 118, 122, 145
Ice Age 98, 122, 156
Ice crystals 127, 141, 146
Ice sheet 98-99, 100, 106, 122-123, 132
Iceberg 100,
Ichthyosaur 16, 17
Idrisi 66, 67
Igloos 144

Iguanodon 4, 8, 9, 11, 12, 29
Incas 76, 77
India 49
Indus Valley 34-35
Inner core 86, 110
Interglacial Age 156
Islands 89, 113
Isobars 137
Itj-towy 42
Jansky, Karl 176
Jansz, Willem 78
Jericho 32
Jet streams 139, 152
Jupiter 162-163, 167
Karla 163
Karnak 47
Keck Telescope 176
Kennedy Space Center 179
Kingsley, Mary 81
Knarrs 65
Knossos, Palace of 33
Kos 53
Kronosaurus 17
Kublai Khan 68, 69
Kush 41
Lagosuchus 5
Lakes 94, 118
Latitude 62, 63
Lava 90, 114
Lawson, William 79
Lesothosaurus 15
Light years 159
Lighthouses 149
Lightning 146-147
Livingstone, David 80, 81
Loch Ness Monster 16
Longisquama 4, 18
Longitude 62
Longships 64
Luxor 47
Macedonia 49
Magellan, Ferdinand 71, 74, 75
Magma 87, 111
Magnetic field 86, 110
Maiasaura 20, 21
Mamenchisaurus 10-11, 16
Mantell, Gideon 8-9, 11
Mantle 86-87, 110-111
Maps 64, 66, 67, 69, 71, 72, 73, 74, 76, 78-79, 81, 82
Mars 162-163, 166-167
Mathematics 153
Maya 38-39

Megalosaurus 8-9
Memphis 42
Mercury 162-163, 165
Meroe 41
Mesopotamia 32
Mesosphere 124
Mesozoic Era 4-5
Metal 86, 105, 106, 110, 131, 132
Meteor shower 171
Meteorite 171
Meteorologists 134, 136, 153, 154
Meteorology 153
Meteors 171
Mexico 38
Mid-Atlantic Ridge 89, 113
Milky Way 160-161, 165
Minerals 88, 105, 112, 131
Minoans 33
Mir Space Station 180, 182
Mohenjo Daro 34-35
Molten rock 93, 117
Monsoons 103, 129, 143
Moons 91, 115, 162-163, 168, 169
Moraine 99, 123
Mosasaurs 30
Mount Olympus 51, 170
Mountains 89, 92-93, 98, 102, 113, 116-117, 122, 128
Mussaurus 21
Mycenaens 33
Napata 41
Natural resources 104, 106 130, 132
Navigation 62-63, 66
Nebulae 160
Neptune 162-163, 166
Newton, Sir Isaac 177
Newton's Laws 176
Nigeria 41
Night 85, 97, 109, 121
Nile, River 42-44, 47
Nimbostratus 140
Nitrogen 124
Nodosaurus 4, 5
Nok 41
North Pole 85, 86, 100, 109, 110, 135
Nuclear power 104, 130
Oasis 96, 120
Ocean floor 89, 113
Oceanography 153
Oceans 88, 94, 103, 105,

112, 118, 129, 131
Oil 104, 130
Oktas 141
Olmecs 38
Olympia 53
Olympic Games 53
Orbits 162-163
Ornitholestes 19
Ornithopods 4, 5
Orodromeus 21
Oudney, Walter 81
Ouranosaurus 25
Outer core 86, 110
Owen, Richard 9
Oxygen 124
Ozone 125
Ozone layer 107, 125, 133, 134, 157
Pachycephalosaurs 4, 30
Pachycephalosaurus 4, 5, 7
Pantheon 59
Parasaurolophus 17
Peary, Robert 82
Per-Ramesses 42
Persian Empire 49
Persians 43, 49
Pharaohs 41-43, 46
Phoenicians 40, 60, 61
Physics 153
Pioneer 182
Pizarro, Franciso 77
Planetariums 182
Planets 162-163
Plateosaurus 6
Plates 86, 110
Plesiosaurs 16, 17
Pliosaur 16, 17
Pluto 162-163, 169
Pole Star 173
Pollution 106, 132
Polo, Marco 68, 69, 73
Polynesians 62
Polyps 89, 113
Pompeii 59
Predictions 154
Prince Henry 70
Prosauropods 6
Protoceratops 20, 21
Proxima Centauri 172
Psittacosaurus 21
Pteranodon 19
Pterosaurs 19
Ptolemy 177
Pulsars 174
Pyramids 41, 44-46

Pythagoras 52
Quadrant 63
Quasars 175
Radars 152
Rain 95, 96, 102-103, 106, 107, 119, 120, 126-127 128-129, 132, 133, 142-143
Rainbows 144
Rainbursts 151
Rainfall 142, 152, 157
Rainforests 103, 106, 129, 132
Rain gauges 142, 154
Ramesses II 47
Recycling 107, 133
Remus 54
Renewable energy 104, 130
Rift valleys 92, 95, 116, 119
Rill 94, 118
Rivers 88, 94-95, 112, 118-119
Rockets 178-179
Rocks 86-87, 95, 96-97, 99, 104, 110-117, 119, 120-121, 123, 130
Roman Empire 42
Romans 40, 48, 54-59
Rome 54-56, 59
Romulus 54
Rosetta Stone 47
Russia 48
Sahara Desert 96, 120
Sailing 139
Sailors 19, 149
Sand 90-1, 96-7, 115-116, 120, 121
Sargon of Akkad 33
Satellites 152, 178-179
Saturn 152, 162-163
Saturn's rings 167
Saurolophus 25
Sauropods 4, 5, 9, 12, 14, 15, 20, 21, 23
Scott, Robert Falcon 82-83
Sea breezes 148-149
Sea of Tranquility 172
Seas 88, 90, 91, 94-95, 96, 102, 106, 112, 114, 115, 118-119, 120, 128, 132
Seasons 103, 129
Seaweed 159
"Seismosaurus" 11
Shang Dynasty 36
Shipping forecasts 153

Shooting stars 171
Showers 154
Silk Route 37, 68-69
Sirius 173
Smiley 163
Snow 93, 94, 98, 100, 117, 118, 122, 126-127 144-145
Snowdrifts 144
Snowfall 150
Snowflakes 144
Soil 86, 106, 110, 132
Solar flares 165
Solar System 84, 108, 162-163, 165, 173
Solid planets 166-167
South Pole 85, 86, 100, 109, 110, 135
Southern Cross 173
Space 158-159
Space probes 166
Spacecraft 178-179
Space Shuttle 178-179, 181
Spain 49, 54
Spaniards 76-77
Sparta 48-50
Speke, John Hanning 80-81
Springs 94, 118
Sputnik I 178
Sputnik II 180
St. Elmo's Fire 147
Stanley, Henry Morton 24, 25
Staple foods 104, 130
Stars 172-173, 174-175
Stegosaurs 4, 14, 23

Stegosaurus 4-5, 12
Stenonychosaurus 22
Stone Age people 60
Storms 127
Stratocumulus 140
Stratopause 134
Stratosphere 124
Stratus 140
Streams 94, 118
Stuart, John 79
Stygimoloch 30
Sudan 40, 43
Sumerians 32-33
Sun 84-85, 102-104, 106-109, 126, 128-129, 130, 132-133, 164-165
Suns 162-163
Sunspots 164
Superclusters 161
Supernovae 174-175
"Supersaurus" 10, 11
Synoptic charts 152
Syria 43
Tanis 42
Tanystropheus 5
Tasman, Abel 78
Telescope 63
Telescopes 8, 12, 24-25
Temperature 102, 125, 128, 157
Temperature, Sun's 164
Teotihuacan 39
Tereshkova, Valentina 28
Thebes 42, 47
Therapods 4, 14
Thermometers 28-29
Thermosphere 124
Thunder 127, 146, 148

Thunderstorms 143, 145, 146-147
Tides 91, 95, 105, 115, 119, 131, 169
Time 176
Time zones 85, 109
Tornadoes 139, 147, 150
Trench, Ocean 89, 113
Tributaries 94, 118
Triceratops 4, 29, 30
Trireme 49
Troodon 21
Tropical regions 135
Tropopause 134
Troposphere 124, 126
Tsintaosaurus 4
Tunis 40
Tuojiangosaurus 23
Turkey 32, 44
Tutankhamun 46-47
Tyrannosaurus rex 4, 5, 6, 12, 13, 14, 19, 23, 30
"Ultrasaurus" 11
Ultraviolet radiation 107, 125, 133
Ultraviolet rays 157
Underground caves 94, 118
Underground spring 96, 120
Universe 84, 104, 108, 158-159
Ur 32
Uranus 8-9, 12
Uruk 32
Valley 89, 113
Valley of the Kings 47
Vehicle Assembly Building 27

Venus 162-163
Vespucci, Amerigo 73
Vikings 62, 64-65, 72
Visibility 149, 152
Volcanoes 89, 90, 92-93, 94, 113, 114, 116-118, 166
Voyager I 167
Wandering stars 175
Water 86, 106, 110, 132
Water cycle 142
Water droplets 142
Water vapor 124, 126-127, 142
Waterfalls 94, 118
Waterspouts 150, 151
Waves 88, 90-1, 105, 112, 114-115, 131
Weather 126-127
Weather forecasters 136
Weather forecasts 152
Weather front 126
Weather stations 152
Weather vanes 154
Weightlessness 181
Wentworth, William 79
White dwarf star 175
Wills, Charles 79
Wind 88, 103, 104, 112, 125, 126, 129, 130, 138-139
Wind direction 154
Wind generators 139
Wind power 139
Wind speed 138, 152
Zeus 51
Zhou Dynasty 36
Ziggurt 32

Created by Zigzag Publishing Ltd,
The Barn, Randolph's Farm,
Brighton Road, Hurstpierpoint,
West Sussex, BN6 9EL, Great Britain.

This edition produced in 1995 for
Barnes & Noble Inc., New York.

Colour separations by RCS Graphics Ltd and
Sussex Repro, Great Britain and Proost, Belgium.

Printed by Midas Printing Ltd, Hong Kong.

This edition contains material previously published
under the titles *100 Questions and Answers about –
Dinosaurs, Ancient Times, Explorers, Planet Earth,
The Sea, Weather* and *Space*.

First published in 1995.

ISBN 1-56619-939-5

10 9 8 7 6 5 4 3 2 1